Torben M. Andersen

Economic Performance

in the Nordic World

Aarhus University Press / The University of Wisconsin Press

The Nordic World
Economic Performance in the Nordic World
© Torben M. Andersen 2021

Cover, layout, and typesetting:
Camilla Jørgensen, Trefold
Cover photograph: Lars Kruse, Aarhus University
Copy editors: Heidi Flegal and Mia Gaudern
Acquisitions editors: Amber Rose Cederström
and Karina Bell Ottosen
This book is typeset in FS Ostro and printed
on Munken Lynx 130 g
Printed by Narayana Press, Denmark
Printed in Denmark 2021

ISBN 978 87 7219 327 4
ISBN 978 0 299 33394 2

This book is available in a digital edition

Library of Congress Cataloging-in-Publication
data is available

Published with the generous support of the
Aarhus University Research Foundation,
the Carlsberg Foundation, and the Nordic
Council of Ministers

The Nordic World series is copublished by
Aarhus University Press and the University
of Wisconsin Press

Aarhus University Press
aarhusuniversitypress.dk

The University of Wisconsin Press
uwpress.wisc.edu

PEER
REVIEWED

MIX
Paper
FSC FSC® C010651

Contents

Chapter 1.
Introduction

The Nordic countries stand out in international comparisons for combining high living standards and low inequality. The system now widely known as the "Nordic welfare model" is quite comprehensive or "extended," including both the social safety net and the public provision of welfare services like care, education, and health services, all of which is financed by taxes, so the total tax revenue constitutes a high share of total income. All these aspects are hallmarks of the Nordic welfare model.

Frequent reference is made to the Nordic welfare model in international policy debates and election campaigns. In 2013 British magazine *The Economist* published an image of a Viking on its front cover to characterize this model as a "supermodel," while a publication from the US government in 2019 characterized it as a "socialist model." In an era with increasing inequality, the Nordic approach to welfare is seen by some as a solution that can accomplish inclusive growth, while for others it means the government playing too large a role. But what characterizes the model? And how is it that the Nordic countries – which are small and highly globalized – have managed to attain such economic success?

The Nordic experience is a puzzle that challenges the standard reasoning in economics textbooks on how the role of the public sector affects economic performance. Such reasoning has its outset in the disincentivizing effects of taxation: Taxes may help reduce inequality, but they distort economic incentives by reducing the after-tax return of various activities. As a consequence, income, employment, and so on are reduced. Lower inequality is achieved at the cost of a less well-performing economy, resulting in lower living standards. According to this standard reasoning, the Nordic countries, with their large public sectors, should not be performing economically on par with, or even better than, similar countries with smaller public sectors and lower taxes. But economic performance in the Nordics is among the best in the world, which is paradoxical in light of the standard reasoning. How can this situation be explained? The purpose of this book is to help answer this puzzling question, and to discuss some of the key challenges to the Nordic welfare model.

Understanding the Nordic experience means developing a more nuanced view of the role of the public sector than that captured by standard reasoning. Taxes may distort economic incentives, but the effect of taxes cannot be seen independently of what taxes are financing and how the economy is structured.

Two aspects are crucial for the economic performance of the Nordic countries. First, the welfare state is not passive. Rather, it is active in improving the opportunities for all to participate in the labor market, which includes searching for jobs and acquiring relevant qualifications to ensure high productivity. This, in turn, supports economic activity. Second, how the market mechanism operates cannot be assessed simply by looking at tax rates. Some public activities may make the market mechanism more efficient, and other types of regulations are also important. Adding to the list of paradoxes, the private sector is at least as liberal in the Nordic countries as it is in many countries with leaner public sectors. Combining a liberal private sector and a large public sector is sometimes called "the third way."

The Nordic paradox is compounded by the fact that these countries are small and open, which supposedly should make it more difficult to reconcile an "extended welfare state" with strong economic performance. However, Nordic policy-makers understand the importance of international competitiveness, and it has long framed policies.

The Nordic welfare model can also be characterized as an employment model. Achieving both high income levels and low income inequality relies on high employment rates – for men and women alike – and a low number of working poor. This is also critical for the financial viability of the model. If employment is low, tax revenues fall and social expenditures rise. Since the model has relatively high levels for both taxes and social benefits, this effect is strong. The financial sustainability of the model therefore depends on maintaining a high employment level in the private sector. It is misleading to characterize the model as a case of "politics against markets," or say that it relies on a decommodification of labor.

The aim of this book is to present some basic insights into the "economics of the Nordic welfare model," which are important in explaining how high income levels, low inequality, and an extended welfare state can coexist. The first part of this book lays out the structure of the Nordic model and provides some data showing how the Nordic countries stand out in a comparative perspective, and it also discusses the concept of welfare models. This is followed by a discussion of the standard view on the economic implications of government activities, and several economic arguments explaining the economic performance of the Nordic countries. The second part of the

9

book looks into specific policy areas, and since this necessitates more detail, this part focuses on the experiences of Denmark: labor market policies (flexicurity), pension systems, and preparations to deal with an aging population. The challenges arising from new technologies and globalization are also discussed. The book concludes by considering what lessons may be learned from the Nordic experience.

The term "Nordic welfare model" is used in the generic sense to denote small, open economies with large public sectors, rather than in the narrow geographical sense. Among the Nordic countries there are significant differences, and historically, only Denmark, Norway, and Sweden were listed as "welfare states," which initially gave rise to the notion of the "Scandinavian welfare model." Later, Finland has been included, and there is an ongoing discussion as to whether Iceland fits this categorization. More recently, Norway can be considered a "special case" due to its large-scale extraction of oil and gas.

Throughout the book, the Nordic countries are compared to the OECD average in order to give a comparative perspective. Clearly, such averages can mask large variations, and in some cases reference is made to specific countries.

Chapter 2.

Economic performance in the Nordic countries

The economic performances of countries can be compared in numerous ways. Such comparisons usually have both a level dimension and a distributional dimension. What is the level of living standard in the country? And how equally are living standards distributed across the population?

Living standards and their distribution profiles can be measured in many ways, but a key variable is income as a measure of material well-being – how much each person or family has at their disposal. Based on this, it is possible to consider both the average income (per capita income) and its distribution. Distributional issues are usually analyzed on the basis of disposable incomes, giving the resources the household has at their disposal; that is, all "market income" (income from labor and capital) less taxes and plus income transfers. In Figure 2.1 these two metrics are used to compare the Nordic countries with the OECD average.[1] This zooms in on the essence of economic performance in the Nordic countries in international com-

1.
The Organisation for Economic Co-operation and Development (OECD) currently has 35 member countries; see www.oecd.org

parison: The income level is high, and incomes are relatively equally distributed.

Figure 2.1 Per capita income and income distribution, Nordic countries and OECD average

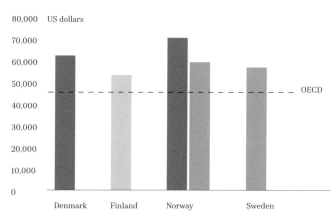

a) Per capita income *

* Per capita income is given as Gross Domestic Product (GDP) per capita, in US dollars at current prices, with current purchasing power parities (PPP) for the year 2019. For Norway, the light brown bar refers to mainland Norway, i.e. excluding offshore activities

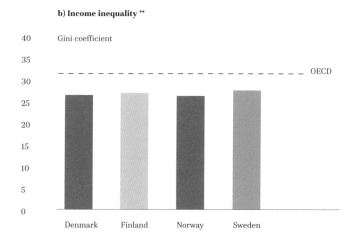

b) Income inequality **

** The Gini coefficient is calculated based on disposable income. The coefficient ranges between 0 and 100; the lower the coefficient, the more equal the income distribution. Data applies to 2018 or closest year for which data are available

Source: www.oecd-ilibrary.org

Two remarks are in order. First, Figure 2.1 gives a snapshot of the situation in 2018, but the same pattern emerges in a longer-term perspective. The Nordic countries have persistently remained among the high-income countries in the OECD, and over time they have not lost ground to, for instance, low-tax countries. Second, in recent years, income inequality has also been increasing in the Nordic countries, as has generally been the case for OECD countries, but it remains low in international comparisons.

Factors other than income and material living conditions are clearly important too, and many comparisons include a broader set of metrics. As an example, the Human Development Index (HDI), compiled by the United Nations (UN), compares living standards based on three key components: per capita income, health measured as life expectancy at birth, and knowledge measured as a weighted average of literacy and school enrollment. The 2018 index ranks Norway as 1, Sweden 8, Denmark 11, and Finland 12, putting them among the best performing countries out of the 189 countries included in the data set.

In international comparisons, the Nordic countries stand out due to their large public sectors, as shown in Figure 3.1. A substantial amount of resources is used or distributed via the public sector. Measured in terms of total public expenditures (or tax revenue), the public sector constitutes about 50 percent of total income (GDP). Put differently, roughly half of the income generated within the economy in a given year is allocated and distributed, one way or another, via the public sector. This is a defining characteristic of the Nordic welfare model. The public sector plays a large role in terms of providing a social safety net and a range of "welfare services," including daycare and care for the elderly, education, and health services, to the entire population. This is elaborated on further in Chapter 3.

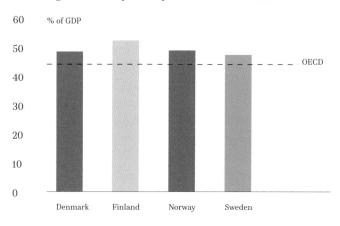

Figure 2.2 Total public expenditure. % of GDP 2019 *

Source: www.oecd-ilibrary.org

* Unweighted OECD average. Notice that the lower tax burden in Norway is not corrected for the revenue from offshore activities

The Nordic countries are small, open economies, and their welfare model has not developed shielded from international competition or market pressure; on the contrary, openness has been a conditioning factor. Openness measured by the "trade share," which shows the importance of foreign trade (export and import) relative to GDP, is above the OECD average. In the past, trade was mainly *intra-industrial*; that is, based on differences in access to natural resources. Denmark was an exporter of agricultural products, while Norway, Sweden, and Finland had comparative advantages in wood and minerals. More recently, trade has become more *inter-industrial*; similar products are made in many countries, although oil and gas are particularly important for Norway. The Nordic countries have adapted to this by developing new comparative advantages in areas such as IT and pharmaceuticals.[2]

From the perspective of ongoing globalization, it is important to note that, historically, the Nordics have faced global competition. While globalization is presently taking on new forms and is perhaps more intense, due to both political decisions (further integration) and technological

2.
Adding to the list of notable differences between the Nordics, Denmark has a large number of small and medium-sized firms, while Sweden has historically had many large firms. Norway and Finland are intermediary cases and have historically been closer to Denmark in this respect

changes (lower information and transport costs), the issue of how to balance social concerns with an internationally competitive economy has a long history, which has become deeply embedded in Nordic policies over the years. The concern with competitiveness has always been a framing factor, based on an understanding that productivity increases are the foundation for real wage growth and high employment. This is encapsulated in what is known as the "Scandinavian model of inflation," which states that wages should first be determined in ("tradeable") sectors facing international competition – like the industrial sector – which would then determine the potential room for wage increases in other ("non-tradeable") sectors – like services and the construction sector. The opposite sequence may jeopardize competitiveness and lead to more cyclical variations, according to this model. Even though reality has not always been in accordance with these principles, they have been anchor points for many years. Naturally, there have been conflicts between labor and capital, but these have been limited by the shared view that safeguarding competitiveness is in the best long-term interest of employers and employees alike.

A premise in many political discussions about the role of the state and markets is the assertion that a large public sector is tantamount to setting market forces aside. This is not a very accurate characterization of the Nordic countries. It is correct that the public sector is not guided by the market mechanism, but that does not imply that the welfare state is "politics against markets." First, many public sector activities such as education and active labor market policies can support work and productivity and thus improve market performance. Second, taxes are important, but it is often overlooked that many other factors influence how the private sector works (and are essential for competitiveness). Markets can be distorted not only by taxes, but also by a lack of competition, excessive bureaucracy, and so on. Therefore, a full and proper analysis of distortions should look beyond taxes and also account for these and other potential distortions. So while the public sectors are large in the Nordic countries, analyses often disregard that their private sectors are among the most liberal in the OECD area. As an example, the OECD product market regulation index, which measures barriers to entry and market competition, assesses countries in terms of "least regulation" and in 2018 ranked Denmark as number 3, Sweden as 6, Norway as 7, and Finland as 17.

To underscore the importance of globalization and competitiveness, Table 2.1 summarizes widely used indices on key aspects related to the private sector, where countries are ranked by performance, from best to worst. Across all three dimensions, the Nordic countries have relatively favorable scores. The Nordic economies are highly globalized, they are business-friendly, and they are competitive.

Table 2.1 Rankings of Nordic countries in Globalization, Ease of doing business, and Competitiveness [*]

	Globalization	Ease of doing business	Competitive business
Denmark	8	4	10
Finland	9	20	11
Norway	12	9	17
Sweden	4	10	8
Number of countries	203	190	141

[*] Globalization measured using the KOF index (2020); see http://globalization.kof.ethz.ch/. Ease of doing business index (2020) compiled by the World Bank; see http://www.doingbusiness.org. Competitiveness index (2019) published by the World Economic Forum; see http://www3.weforum.org/docs/WEF_TheGlobalCompetitivenessReport2019.pdf

The Nordic countries build on a strong corporatist tradition, with close cooperation between employer organizations and trade unions. Many labor market issues are settled by the labor market organizations, examples being minimum wages in Denmark and Sweden. Unionization is high, and although it has recently been declining, agreements reached as a result of "collective bargaining" between employers and employees cover most workers.

The level of trust in the Nordic countries is high, and this also holds true for public institutions. Corruption is low, and transparency in public administration is high. Both these factors are conducive to support for collective arrangements – people expect that the money paid in taxes is put to proper use, as discussed in Chapter 3. It has been suggested that particular norms are prevalent in the Nordic countries that make it easier to implement collective solutions. This is debatable, but it should be noted that there are many checks and balances in the system, which also raises "Big Brother" issues. As an example, a wide variety of personal data on individuals, ranging from income to health conditions, is registered on different public systems that all use personal identification numbers (which is why we have such detailed, individualized data in the Nordic countries).

Lessons from the Nordics

High incomes, low inequality, and large public sectors have characterized the Nordic countries for the last four or five decades. These specific characteristics are persistent, and it is noteworthy that they have prevailed against a background of quite significant changes in economic structure, including technological advances and globalization.

Public debates often proclaim particular countries as "superstars," as has been the case for Germany, Sweden, and, more recently, Denmark. While there are surely differences in countries' economic performances and lessons to be learned from "cross-country" benchmarking, such discussions easily become superficial, leading to a naive "copy and paste" view that attributes the favorable economic performance of a country to a few policy facts, and takes it for granted that they can be easily adopted and successful in other countries. This neglects the complementarity between different policy instruments, the country's institutional structure, and its political environment (Moene 2016). History also documents that the economic superstars have had their ups and downs, stressing that performance is shock-dependent and various models/countries have different comparative advantages. The Nordic model is not crisis-free. There have been several deep crises, notably in the 1980s and 1990s, when unemployment soared and public finances were on an unsustainable course, and the future of the Nordic welfare model looked bleak (Lundberg 1985; Lindbeck et al. 1993). Clearly, the Nordics have also been affected by global crises like the bursting of the IT bubble, the financial crisis, and, more recently, the COVID-19 pandemic.

The future of the Nordic welfare model is often questioned, and its near-demise predicted, for a long list of reasons, including globalization, migration, and aging populations. It is noteworthy that the Nordic countries have proven an ability to undertake reforms to overcome these crises (Andersen, Bergman, & Hougaard Jensen 2015). A common denominator of these reforms has been adapting policies to ensure that the overall objectives of the welfare state can be reached. Rather than any specific policy details, this ability to reform is an important characteristic, and it builds on a strong tradition of consensus-seeking and trust.

Chapter 3.

The Nordic welfare model

The welfare state is commonly understood in broad terms as the norms, institutions, and rules in a society that aim to correct the outcome of an unregulated market economy in a more egalitarian direction. Concepts like "justice" and "fairness" are crucial in discussions about the scope of, and the need for, the welfare state. Notions like "welfare" and "social models" are frequently used in policy debates and cross-country comparisons, but the precise meaning of this concept varies, and so do the underlying principles in terms of social rights and entitlements, as well as the size and structure of the public sector.

Welfare regimes

A useful distinction between three different types of welfare states, also called "welfare models" or "welfare regimes," was introduced by Esping-Andersen (1990).[3] The prototype welfare models are: (a) the residual/liberal/ Anglo-Saxon model; (b) the corporatist/conservative/continental European model; and (c) the universal/social democratic/Nordic model. These models differ in the weight they give to the market, to civil society (family, church,

3.
This classification has been contested, and various more refined classifications have been proposed. However, it is a useful framework for considering key properties of welfare arrangements

19

friends, private organizations, and so on), and to the state in dealing with citizens' adverse life events and providing social services. No country fits exactly into the prototype welfare regimes defined by Esping-Andersen, but the taxonomy captures important difference between countries. The US is close to the liberal model; Germany to the corporatist model; and Denmark – and the other Nordic countries – to the universal model.

In the liberal or Anglo-Saxon model, the state plays a residual role in the sense of providing an ultimate "floor" in cases where the market or civil society do not suffice. State-provided benefits are modest, and concerns about work incentives play a dominant role.

The corporatist or continental European model relies on status and the family as the backbone of society, and therefore also as providers of social services. In its modern form, mandatory insurance systems play a crucial role, and they are mostly tied to personal labor-market status. The activities of the state tend to be directed towards families rather than individuals.

The universal or Nordic model builds on the principle of "universal social rights for all" – that is, a person's eligibility for welfare services is individual and independent of contributions and social status. The welfare arrangement has two key pillars: the "social safety net," offering income support to people unable to support themselves, and the "provision of basic welfare services" like education, health services, and care. Importantly, the social safety net is intended to ensure a decent living standard for those without an earned income, and the welfare services provided should live up to contemporary standards and meet the reasonable requirements of most people. The public solution is not a second-rate solution used only by those who cannot afford otherwise; it is meant to be used by all. Welfare arrangements are financed via various types of taxes, and this is an important collective trait of the model.

This makes the universal welfare model individual and collective at the same time. Rights and entitlement are defined at the individual level, while responsibility and thus financing rest at the collective level. This can also be interpreted in terms of a common pool – where everyone contributes tax payments to the welfare state, depending on their ability to pay, which in turn depends on their income, consumption, wealth, and so on. Independently of contributions, the individual has access to welfare services like education and healthcare, and is covered by the social safety net. This setting clearly raises political questions about the role of the state, but from an economic perspective it also has both pros and cons, which will be discussed below.

A brief history

To provide an overview of the development in public sector size, Figure 3.1 shows an aggregate measure of the size of the public sector in terms of total tax revenue (as a share of GDP). The figure includes the Nordic countries, with the US as a representative of the liberal model and Germany as a representative of the corporatist model. For comparison, the OECD average is also included.

In the mid-1950s, there were hardly any differences in public sector sizes across OECD countries (Lindert 2004; Lindbeck 1997). The differences evolved during the 1960s and 1970s due to the influences of political structures and institutions, and economic factors. Since the mid-1980s there has not been much change, and the differences across countries have persisted; countries made different choices, as illustrated in Figure 3.1, and their different welfare states have become mature or persistent. Current differences in public sector sizes match the classification of welfare models given above. The Nordic countries have large public sectors, the US a small public sector, and Germany an intermediately sized public sector.

The persistent differences in public sector size since the 1980s are noteworthy in the context of the argument that globalization and other forces create a pressure towards convergence to one of the three prototypes discussed above. No such convergence has taken place, and if anything the persistent cross-country differences are more striking. This is discussed further in Chapter 7.

Figure 3.1 Total tax revenue as a share of GDP, 1955–2019 *

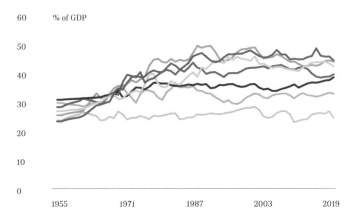

* The decline in the tax revenue share in Norway is explained by the growing importance of the oil/gas sector

| Denmark | Finland | Norway | Sweden |
| Germany | UK | USA | |

Sources: OECD Revenue Statistics 2007 (1955–65), www.oecd-ilibrary.org (1965–2018)

Numerous explanations have been offered for the growth of the public sector in general, and for public sector growth in the Nordic welfare model in particular (Pestieau & Lefebvre 2018). Changes in society are an important driver. Industrialization implied a growth in paid labor and introduced new risks, such as unemployment. It was accompanied by urbanization, affecting family structures and local communities. This process created a need for institutions to address individuals' adverse life events like unemployment and illness, as well as a need for new forms of insurance and protection. The late nineteenth and early twentieth centuries saw the rise of insurance arrangements for work injuries, sickness, unemployment, and pensions. These arrangements were gradually expanded, but most of the expansion took place in the latter half of the twentieth century, when the welfare states, as we known them today, were born.

However, functionalist explanations for the growth of the public sector cannot stand alone. Across OECD countries, which are otherwise similar in many respects, welfare models differ significantly, as seen in Figure 3.1. Political and institutional factors are clearly important. Specifically for the Nordic model, one explanation is that smaller and more homogenous countries have had more scope to develop "collective" solutions. Differences in norms and culture are other possible explanatory factors. Religion has also been offered as an explanation, based on the fact that comprehensive or "extended" welfare states are seen in predominantly Protestant countries, Protestantism being associated with a strong work ethic. It is beyond the scope of this book to offer a detailed discussion of these factors, and the following focuses on the economic aspects of the model.

The welfare state is often characterized in terms of the size of the public sector, as shown above, and there is a tendency to focus on this aspect because it is relatively easily measurable. Two caveats are important. Firstly, public intervention can take on many other forms beyond taxes and expenditures, not least: rules and regulations. The latter may be as important as the former, or even more important, but they are often neglected, as discussed above. Secondly, and crucially, other institutions, not least in the labor market, play a vital role in how social problems are

addressed and solved. Given the role of labor market organizations, "welfare society" may be a better term for the
Nordic model than "welfare state." To avoid confusion, the
following uses the term "the Nordic welfare model."

Public sector structure

The Nordic welfare model rests on two pillars: the
social safety net, and the provision of welfare services. In
addition it handles classic public sector activities like administration, the judicial system, the police, the military,
and so on.

Historically, the expansion of the public sector
during the 1960s and 1970s can roughly be divided into
two phases. First, public expenditure and thus the provision of welfare services rose, driven by expansions in public education, healthcare, and so forth. Second, the social
safety net was expanded and its expenditures increased
in the wake of the crisis in the 1970s triggered by oil price
increases. A snapshot of the current expenditure levels
in terms of social expenditures (various types of income
transfers) and public consumption (activities performed
by the public sector) is given in Figure 3.2.

Figure 3.2 Social expenditures and public consumption

a) Social expenditures *

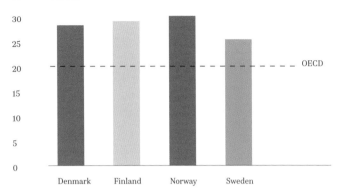

b) Public consumption **

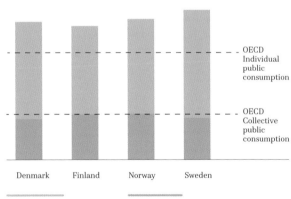

Source: www.oecd-ilibrary.org

25

Social safety net

The social safety net includes a variety of benefit types covering different adverse life events. All citizens[4] are entitled to financial support (the universalistic principle applies), which should be at a level offering decent living standards to those incapable of supporting themselves and their family, as described below. The extent of the social safety net is illustrated in Figure 3.2 (a) in terms of resources spent as a share of GDP. As expected, the Nordic countries have higher social expenditures than is generally observed across OECD countries.

The social safety net has three key elements: (a) pensions, (b) income-replacing transfers, and (c) purpose-targeted transfers. Historically, pensions have been an important element of the welfare state, and they are discussed further in Chapter 6.

In international comparisons, the design of the social safety net in the Nordic countries stands out in several respects.

First, entitlement is a universal right, and therefore, in principle, all citizens are covered. Those unable to support themselves due to unemployment, sickness, or loss of work capability are entitled to some form of support. This reflects a distributional concern to ensure that everyone can maintain a minimum living standard, but it also has an insurance function. Income may be lost due to reasons outside one's own control, and the social safety net is an insurance against too large a drop in income. The coverage of the social safety net is broad, and therefore most people who are unable to support themselves are entitled to some form of "transfer income."

Second, transfers are relatively generous. The generosity of the social safety net can be measured by the "replacement ratio," which shows benefit level relative to the wage if employed. It is a characteristic of the Nordic

4.
This is subject to residence principles; see Chapter 7

countries that replacement ratios are high for low-income groups, while they are not particularly high for average – or high-income groups. This reflects distributional priorities, but it also raises a classic problem. On the one hand, few people fall below the poverty line, but on the other hand, work incentives are reduced. If the decrease in net income in case of job loss is small due to generous benefits, it follows that the income gain if returning to work is small.

Thirdly, a related issue is that while the system has some universalistic traits in the sense that eligibility is an individual right independent of contributions and status, it is important to point out that eligibility is not unconditional. For individuals of working age, there is a strong focus on the ability to be self-supporting. Therefore, a person's eligibility is subject to a number of conditionalities. These are known as "active labor market policies" or "workfare," which include requirements for active job searching, participation in education programs, job training, and so on (see Chapter 5). An active labor market policy has the dual purpose of enhancing qualifications and employability, and strengthening job-search incentives.

Hence, the social safety net in the Nordic welfare model does not offer an unconditional basic income or a "demogrant" for all. For people considered capable of working (and below the pension age), the system is an insurance system covering temporary loss of income in case of adverse life events like unemployment and illness, but it is not a passive or permanent support program that makes work unnecessary. The Nordic welfare model is an employment model, as discussed further in Chapter 4.

In assessing the role of benefits for income distribution, the time dimension is important. Persons/families may have a low income in a given year, without permanently having a low income. This is the case for university students, for instance, who tend to have higher incomes later in life, and for the self-employed, who often have volatile incomes. Measuring income inequality based on lifetime incomes reduces inequality considerably, compared to measures based on annual income. Equally importantly, programs may have very different effects depending on whether they are assessed on an annual or lifetime basis. As an example, study grants reduce income inequality in a given year, but may increase it in a lifetime perspective, since the support is given to individuals who achieve high lifetime incomes. Conversely, a transfer such as a disability pension would reduce both annual income inequality and lifetime inequality, since individuals with a severely reduced working capacity have low lifetime earned income.

The fact that redistribution is high in the Nordic countries, even though the underlying inequality in market incomes is low, points to another puzzle. According to standard economic-policy reasoning[5], a more unequal distribution of incomes (measured by the ratio of mean income to median income) should increase the political support for more redistribution. Empirically, more political support for redistribution is not observed in countries with a higher underlying level of inequality. The Nordic countries are a case in point: Inequality in market income is low, yet there is still strong support for redistributive policies.

5.
A rational theory of the size of government. *Journal of Political Economy*, 89, 914–927

Provision of welfare services

Total expenditures on public sector activities as a share of GDP are shown in Figure 3.2 (b). In national accounts, these expenditures are termed "public consumption" and comprise wage expenditures, acquisitions from private companies, and so on. These expenditures are split between "collective public consumption" and "individual public consumption." The former refers to the classic public sector activities (administration, legal system, police, military, and so on), and in the Nordic countries such expenditures are on par with the OECD average.

Individual public consumption refers to expenditures on the so-called welfare services. These services are provided to specific individuals and therefore termed "individual public consumption." Welfare services include childcare, education, health services, and old-age care. They are tax-financed and therefore generally free of charge for the user. Access is universal and thus basically needs-determined. This is noteworthy, since universality is usually discussed in the context of the social safety net. And as noted earlier, the publicly provided services are not meant to be a second-rate solution used only by those who cannot afford other alternatives. They are meant to be used by all, and to comply with contemporary standards.

What makes the Nordic countries stand out in international comparison is their extensive provision of welfare services, as shown in Figure 3.2 (b). These expenditures constitute about two thirds of total public consumption.

Since access is based on universalism, service provision contributes to redistribution and equality beyond what is captured by standard income measures, as used, for instance, in Figure 2.1. Access to free education or healthcare clearly matters more to low-income families than to high-income families. For all OECD countries, the public provision of services contributes to a reduction in inequality; that is, there is a progressive element in welfare provision. However, in relative terms, the reduction in inequality is larger in the Nordic countries than in other countries, due to the large role welfare services play in the welfare model.

The universal principle should also be seen in the context of equal opportunities. Private financing of activities like education implies a strong social gradient in who can access these activities. However, there is no guarantee that the most able children will be born to rich parents, and therefore private financing can imply a locking-in of talent. Collective financing reduces such financial barriers to gaining access to education. This benefits individuals, but it also benefits society in general, by generating more "human capital," which is important for production and incomes.

Other expenditure types also have potential effects on economic performance. Daycare and old-age care make it easier for women to participate in the labor market, education enhances labor force participation and productivity, and healthcare activities are also important to the labor force. These effects are discussed in more detail in Chapter 4, but the general point here is that the importance of taxes cannot be seen independently of what they are financing.

Financing

The welfare states of the Nordic countries are financed by taxes levied on consumption, income, and wealth, as well as excise taxes. Tax structure is complicated in all the Nordic countries, and it is beyond the scope of this book to give all the details. However, a number of key facts are important.

First, the dominant source of revenue accrues from taxation of earned income, either when it is earned or when it is spent. Revenue from the taxation of corporations and capital constitutes less than 15 percent of total revenue. In policy discussions, it is sometimes asserted that the welfare state taxes capital to the benefit of labor – the classic class conflict – but this is not an accurate description of the Nordic welfare model.

Second, the tax system has progressive elements; that is, a higher tax rate applies to high incomes compared to low incomes. However, the degree of progression has been reduced in recent years, to reduce high marginal taxes and thereby strengthen work incentives. At the same time, tax bases have been extended by reducing some deductions, most importantly, for instance, for mortgage interest payments. In general, these deductions are important for high-income groups, and hence this has contributed to more redistribution.

Thirdly, in a given year, public revenue does not have to balance expenditures; deficits and surpluses are possible. A key reason why differences between revenues and expenditures may arise in a given year is an effect called the "automatic budget reaction." When taxes depend on income and thus employment, and when expenditures like unemployment benefits depend on unemployment, it follows that the budget balance (revenue less expenditures) automatically improves when economic activity goes up (a business cycle upturn), and deteriorates when economic activity goes down (a business cycle downturn).

The automatic budget reaction is the outcome of the design of the tax system and the social safety net. At the individual level, these programs provide insurance, and in case of aggregate changes, such as an increase in the unemployment rate during a recession, they add up to economy-wide effects. This stabilizes the disposable incomes of households and therefore aggregate demand, which in turn may stabilize economic activity. In a business cycle upturn, the automatic budget reaction drags purchasing power out of the economy, helping to cool it off, and vice versa in a business cycle downturn. These effects are also known as the "automatic stabilizers." Since the public sector is large, with a high tax share and a generous social safety net, the cyclical dependency of the budget is large – and the automatic stabilizers are strong. However, fiscal space is required for these stabilizers to work. This means that policy-makers should ensure that public finances are consolidated in economically good times, such that there is room for deficits in bad times. If the budget is in deficit even in normal times and debt is high, the automatic budget reaction may induce a fiscal crisis in the event of an economic downturn. Financial market responses leading to higher interest rates on the debt may fuel a debt spiral, forcing policy-makers to tighten fiscal policy in a situation where the opposite is needed to stabilize employment and income. In other words, to reap the beneficial effects of the automatic stabilizers, fiscal discipline is needed. The Nordic countries experienced this during crisis years in the 1970s and 1980s, when deep economic crises also led to public debt crises. Therefore, in more recent times, they have been front-runners in pursuing fiscal consolidation to ensure sufficient room for the automatic stabilizers to work.

Policy-makers may be tempted to postpone the financing of expenditures – as expenditure increases are usually popular, and tax increases unpopular. This may create a deficit bias, causing systematic deficits and growing debt, since unpopular consolidations are postponed. However, as discussed above, this may hamper the ability to stabilize the economy. It is worth stressing that deficit bias does not characterize the Nordic countries. There have been periods of systematic deficits due to prolonged crisis, but debt levels have subsequently been reduced. As an example, Denmark and Sweden were among the few countries to bring their debt level down both before and after the financial crisis in 2008 and also prior to the outbreak of COVID-19 in 2020, and they are also among the countries that are best prepared for an aging population, as discussed in Chapter 6. The global pandemic has highlighted the importance of fiscal prudence in normal times. Lockdowns and various regulations to contain the virus have been accompanied by financial support to employers and employees, and there has not been a binding financing constraint for these measures. This can be interpreted as an extension of the social safety net to cover an unusual type of event, but also as an investment in keeping production capacity and job matches intact until the health situation allows a phasing-out of the restrictions.

One Nordic model?

Despite the concept of a Nordic welfare model, a careful study of policies in the Nordic countries reveals some striking differences. There are no unique approaches or solutions adopted in the Nordic countries; the key policy instruments do not differ in any significant respects from those applied in other countries. It is not the ingredients that make a difference. It is the entire package.

There are notable differences among the Nordic countries in the specific policy design of their welfare policies and their financing. For instance, Denmark and Sweden have chosen very different paths in designing their pension systems (see Chapter 7). Unemployment insurance is voluntary in Denmark, Finland, and Sweden, but mandatory in Norway. At the macro level the Nordic countries feature a range of monetary regimes, with Norway and Sweden having floating exchange rates (inflation targeting), Denmark pursuing a unilateral peg to the euro, and Finland being a euro country. Denmark, Finland, and Sweden are members of the European Union (EU), but Norway is not (although it is associated as a country in the European Economic Area, or EEA). Although the total tax share is high in the Nordic countries, tax structures differ, with Denmark having the largest share of tax revenue accruing from direct income taxes and value added tax (VAT), while Sweden, for example, raises much more tax revenue from "social contributions" paid by employers and/or employees.

These differences in specific policy designs underline a crucial point: The entire package matters more than the specific ingredients. The overall objectives and aims are essential, but they can be reached in different ways. It is also noteworthy that the Nordic countries have seen a series of successive reforms and changes – and the Nordic model was not created once-and-for-all, sometime in the past (Valkonen & Vihriälä 2014). Rather, it is dynamically evolving alongside various changes in society. But all along, the main characteristics outlined in Chapter 2 have been maintained.

The Nordic experience shows that the naive "copy and paste" perspective often taken in comparative policy discussions, which focus on a single or a few policy instruments, is misleading; it overlooks the interdependencies between the different policy elements.

The Nordic model should not be defined or assessed in terms of specific policy instruments; what matters are the overarching objectives. These have remained stable over time, while the specific policies and instruments used to achieve the objectives differ across time and countries, as discussed in later chapters.

Chapter 4.

The economics of the welfare model

Reconciling the economic performances of the Nordic countries with the fact that their public sectors and thus their tax burdens are large raises a fundamental question, or perhaps even a paradox. How is it possible to square a concern for equity and welfare provision with a well-functioning economy when this implies a large public sector and consequently high taxes? The Nordic countries appear to be a sort of "economic bumblebee" – which really should not be able to fly.

The theoretical arguments

Standard economic theory predicts that an extended welfare model comes at a cost, in terms of economic performance. While, on the one hand, high taxes may finance the provision of welfare services and a social safety net, leading to lower inequality, they will, on the other hand, distort economic incentives. High taxes lower the return on enterprise, education, and work, and therefore, according to this view, an extended welfare state should come at the cost of a less well-performing economy and less affluence. There is a trade-off between a well-functioning economy (efficiency) and distribution (equity). Or to put it differently: When the pie is divided more equally, the pie will shrink. This theory focuses on the negative incentive effects that follow from the taxes and transfers needed to accomplish a more equal distribution of income. The US economist Arthur Okun dubbed this the "big trade-off," explaining it with the metaphor of a leaky bucket: "The money must be carried from the rich to the poor in a leaky bucket. Some of it will simply disappear in transit, so the poor will not receive all the money that is taken from the rich" (Okun 1975:91).

The standard economics textbook bases its theoretical reasoning on a frictionless economy with perfectly competitive markets. Price signals guide the decisions of firms and consumers, and the resulting outcome satisfies the so-called Pareto criterion. This criterion says that it is impossible to suggest an alternative allocation of resources that will put some in a better situation without leaving others in a worse situation. The outcome is, in this sense, efficient: There are no "free lunches." Importantly, this does not imply that the outcome is fair. The implied income distribution is not necessarily politically acceptable, and therefore policy-makers can use transfers and taxes to shift the distribution in a more acceptable direction. However, taxes distort economic incentives. The return to the private decision-maker is the after-tax value, which is obviously lower than the before-tax value (the economic value to society or "social value"). Taxes create a wedge between the private return and the "social return"; the higher the tax rate, the larger the wedge. Private decision-makers respond to the after-tax return, and therefore economic incentives are distorted by taxes. This applies generally, whether the decision is how much to work, or whether to get an education or move for a new

6.
This assumes that
there are no "exter-
nalities" (external
factors exerting an
influence which
is not reflected in
prices or costs). If
there is a negative
externality due
to e.g. pollution,
the private return
is larger than
the social return,
and a tax, e.g. on
pollution, may
change incen-
tives in a socially
desirable direction.
This is called Pigou
taxation

job. In short, the private return (the after-tax return)[6] is lower than the social return (the before-tax return), and therefore economic activity is sub-optimally low. This may imply a lower employment level, lower income, and so on, which is illustrated in Figure 4.1. Where to position the country on this trade-off is a political choice.

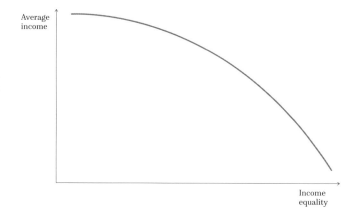

Figure 4.1 Trade-off between efficiency and equity
– perfect markets

There is another explanation of big government and its negative effects on economic performance. Government may grow in a political process driven by self-interest and "rent-seeking" activities to maximize personal gain. Interest groups may push projects that yield them well-defined benefits, while the costs are shared via taxation by the general population (Buchanan & Musgrave 1999). The political process fosters a tendency for policy-makers to promote "pork barrel" projects that only benefit a particular subset of the population, such as infrastructure projects that do not have a large economic return. Moreover, bureaucracy and rent-seeking activities may reinforce these mechanisms and create a tendency for the public sector to grow. In the US, phrases like "feeding the beast" and "starving the beast" are often used in discussions about the public sector and taxes to signal that taxes do not finance activities that are beneficial to the average citizen, but are used on administration and rent-seeking activities. To sum up, this line of reasoning has the same implications as the classical view: that a larger public sector is tantamount to more bureaucracy and rent-seeking activities, which in turn leads to a less well-functioning economy. This is not how the public sector is perceived in the Nordic countries – quite the opposite; the public sector and its institutions enjoy a high level of trust in these countries. One indicator of this is Transparency International's index on corruption (including 183 countries)[7], which, for 2018, had Denmark ranked first, Finland and Sweden ranked a split third, and Norway ranked seventh. A common-sense assessment also shows that bureaucracy and rent-seeking cannot be an overriding problem in the Nordic countries; if their governments were large and very inefficient, it would be hard to explain their favorable economic performance.

Neither the classical economic view nor the bureaucracy-based view captures the Nordic experience. This does not render these lines of reasoning irrelevant, but it highlights the point that there must be some countervailing factors at play in the Nordic countries.

One alternative, the intervention or "market-failure" view, holds that an unregulated market economy does not fit the idealized model of competitive markets ensuring a Pareto-efficient outcome. Market failures can arise due to information problems, transactions costs, and externalities, and they make the market mechanism work less efficiently, due to a lack of competition (market power) and constraints on market opportunities (credit constraint) (Atkinson 1999; Sandmo 1998).

A properly designed public intervention may mitigate some of these failures and therefore lead to simultaneous improvements in average income and income

7.
See https://www.transparency.org/cpi2018

38

equality. This is illustrated in Figure 4.2. and discussed in more detail below. Starting from the laissez-faire situation without any policy intervention (point A), intervention that mitigates market failures may both increase income and make the income distribution more equal (moving up along the A-B segment). However, by continued intervention, eventually a point like B is reached, and further intervention strikes a trade-off where more equality in the distribution of income (less inequality) comes at the cost of less average income (the B-C segment). What causes the turning point is that the marginal gains from further interventions are declining, while the marginal costs of tax financing are increasing. Importantly, the path illustrated in Figure 4.2. does not apply to all forms of policy interventions; it illustrates a case with an intervention that is properly targeted to remedy market imperfections (some examples of which are discussed below).

Figure 4.2 Trade-off between efficiency and equity – intervention in the presence of market failures

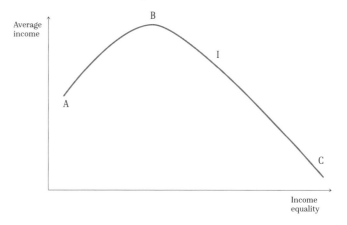

Figures 4.1 and 4.2 encapsulate very different views on the public sector or the welfare state. The standard view (Figure 4.1) is that if the market outcomes are not

considered acceptable, policy-makers can intervene to "repair" the situation, but this comes at a cost in terms of a less well-functioning market (efficiency loss). The market-failure view (Figure 4.2) is that policies that address problems arising due to market failures may, within a certain range, both improve average income (efficiency) and make the distribution of incomes more equal (equity).

The hump-shaped curve depicted in Figure 4.2 has further important implications. If policy-makers are concerned about average income *and* about its distribution, it would never be optimal to choose policies that position the economy on the segment between A and B. An intervention moving the economy at least to point B would be associated with more income and less income inequality; a win–win situation. Moving beyond point B to the segment between B and C, policy-makers encounter a trade-off between average income and its distribution. In general, it would be optimal to move to this segment, unless the level of inequality associated with point B is considered optimal.

The reasoning above gives important insights into some key policy questions. Suppose a country is positioned at point I on the curve. In this case, two different questions may be asked. The broader question is: What are the consequences of the welfare state (intervention) compared to no welfare arrangements at all? And the narrower question is: What happens if the intervention is expanded or contracted, just slightly?

The broader question compares a hypothetical situation with and without intervention, or makes a comparison across countries with different levels of welfare states (intervention). Specifically, comparing point A (no intervention) to point I (the outcome with intervention) shows that the latter has higher average income, lower income inequality, and a larger public sector (more intervention). This helps to explain the Nordic paradox – that countries with a large public sector can also have high income and low inequality if the welfare state is successfully targeting various market failures (Andersen 2015). More generally, cross-country comparisons involve countries on both the A-B and B-C segments (and some positioned below the frontier given by the graph A-B-C). Countries may be positioned differently for various historical, institutional, and political reasons. The overall outcome therefore depends on how well interventions are targeted, and on institutional structure and political decisions.

The next matter is the narrower question of the effects of a "slight" policy change, that is, a small movement on the B-C segment in the upward or downward direction. Here, there is clearly a trade-off: more equality is attained at the cost of lower average income or vice versa. Hence, even though the welfare state delivers higher average income and lower income inequality, this does not mean that trade-off concerns become irrelevant.

The insights summarized in Figure 4.2 give a guide to cross-country comparisons. First, as shown in Figure 2.1, the Nordic countries stand out from the OECD average by having both higher average income and lower inequality. The average OECD country does not even reach the B-C segment on the frontier. Examples would include France and Spain, which have lower per capita income and higher income inequality than the Nordic countries. For other countries, the comparison is less clear. For example, the US and Switzerland have higher average income but also higher income inequality than the Nordic countries. They are all at different positions on the B-C segment of the curve. A trade-off exists between average income and inequality: Is the lower inequality in the Nordic countries worth the lower average income when compared to the US or Switzerland? This question is clearly political. Obviously, many more dimensions can be brought into cross-country comparisons, but the examples above reflect the fundamental questions.

The following sections discuss how some key welfare state activities should be seen in relation to market failures, explaining relations like the one illustrated in Figure 4.2.

Social insurance

Most discussions about the Nordic welfare states focus on redistribution. This follows directly from the classical view on the trade-off between efficiency and equity (Figure 4.1) and the fact that many welfare policies are, indeed, redistributive. These redistributive characteristics derive from society attending to the sick, those unable to work, those unable to find work, and so on, and these activities are financed by those who are healthy, able to work, and have jobs. The design of the social safety net, welfare services, and the tax system all contribute to redistribution.

On further reflection, it is difficult to separate redistribution from insurance. The redistribution interpretation of welfare arrangements refers to an *ex post* situation; that is, when we know who is sick and who is healthy, we know who will receive from the system and who will contribute to it. However, taking an *ex ante* view, there is some risk involved in determining one's position at a later point in time, and welfare arrangements perform an insurance function. A given individual does not know whether they will become ill, but they know that if it happens, the public healthcare system will provide for them. Likewise, if the ability to work is lost, the social safety net is there, and so on for various adverse life events. Even tax payments include an insurance element, since more taxes are paid if a person's income turns out to be high, and less if it turns out to be low. Hence, seen from an *ex ante* perspective, welfare arrangements provide insurance in relation to various possible adverse circumstances that may arise in a person's life (Barr 2001). This can be termed "implicit" or "social" insurance.

Private markets do offer insurance options, via explicit insurance markets and more generally via financial markets, for example by saving to build up a buffer so negative events like unemployment and sickness can be accommodated. However, insuring all forms of risk in the market is difficult, costly, and in some cases impossible, and there are many potential reasons for market failures, especially when it comes to insuring labor income.

The basic idea of insurance is risk diversification: The risks do not disappear, but the consequences are shared. Risk diversification can be achieved via an explicit insurance contract (such as fire insurance on your house) or be included as part of an employment contract (such as payment for a certain period of sick leave), and in many other ways. In an explicit insurance contract, all customers pay a premium *ex ante* to be covered against a particular risk or event, and those who, *ex post*, experience the event get compensation. Note that a private insurance contract has *ex post* redistribution – those who are affected by the event receive a net compensation financed by the net contributions paid by all those who are not affected.

While the basic principles are simple, insurance is difficult in practice, due to the cost of acquiring information and transaction costs. How do we observe whether the event has happened? Can the individual affect the probability that the event might happen, and its consequences? Will only those who have a high probability of being exposed to the event buy the contract? The first question points to an incentive problem (known in the literature as "moral hazard"), since the contract shifts responsibility from the customer to the insurance company, and the individual does not carry all the consequence of decisions taken (as is also the case with the "social insurance" aspect of taxation). The last question refers to what are known as "adverse selection" problems being particularly severe for insurance markets. It is evident that insurance becomes difficult if the majority of those buying the insurance contract have a (high) probability of being affected by the insured event. Adverse selection can result in poorly functioning insurance markets, or even preclude insurance. An additional issue is that insurance contracts must be made before knowing whether one has a low or high probability of being affected by the event. A major constraint is that private insurance relies on explicit contracts, which are difficult to make early in life, not only since explicit contracts cannot be entered into before a certain age (typically 18), but also because of people's inability to pay for insurance early in life.

Market failures are a necessary condition to justify public intervention, but they are not sufficient in themselves. The problems do not necessarily disappear when social insurance is substituted for private insurance. Social insurance must be well targeted to remedy the market failures. There are several reasons why social insurance can accomplish more risk diversification than private markets. One is the possibility of encompassing the entire population, which eliminates the adverse selection that poses particular problems for insurance markets. Moreover, social insurance covers individuals from birth. Via the public budget, risk can be shared across time and thus across generations, which is not possible via private markets. Finally, social insurance is portable in the sense that coverage is not tied to a particular job or location, which is conducive to flexibility in the labor market.

If private insurance markets suffer from market failures, the basic premise underlying the classical view discussed above does not hold true. However, a properly designed intervention can remedy this. As argued above, the welfare state can be interpreted as a large, encompassing insurance arrangement that works via the social safety net, welfare service provision, and taxation. These arrangements cannot be assessed solely in terms of how their financing affects incentives; the insurance effects have to be taken into account, and this produces a situation like the one depicted in Figure 4.2. Clearly, this gives a different perspective on the role of the welfare state.

Social insurance may have two types of effects. If people dislike risk – as most people do – access to insurance has a direct, positive effect on welfare. The risks do not disappear, but you know there is some insurance mechanism if something like unemployment or illness happens to strike you – and this improves welfare.

Insurance may also affect incentives by making individuals more willing to take risks (the flexicurity argument; see Chapter 5). If the economic consequence of losing your job is smaller, due to social insurance mechanisms, you might be more willing to accept jobs in which there is a high lay-off risk, or be less concerned about the effects of globalization or new technologies, since you know that you are not carrying the costs alone. In short, social insurance may be conducive to flexibility and adaptability in the labor market, which in turn may strengthen the private sector and lead to higher levels of income.

The "cradle-to-grave" model

The Nordic welfare model is often portrayed as a "cradle-to-grave" model. This is captured in Figure 4.3, which shows the average net transfers from the welfare state to the individual at different ages. These net transfers are the value of services and transfers received, net of taxes paid. There is a clear life-cycle pattern in net contributions. The young are net beneficiaries (through child-care and education), the middle-aged are net contributors (they work and pay taxes), and the elderly are net beneficiaries (through pensions, health services, and old-age care). This can be interpreted from a three-generation perspective: children, parents, and grandparents. In a very broad sense, parents (the working-age population) provide the financial basis on which the welfare state can provide for children and grandparents. This is termed the "intergenerational contract" or "social contract," around which the welfare state is built.

In somewhat oversimplified terms, before industrialization and urbanization, the family and local civil society displayed the same generational linkage, with three families living under the same roof. As a response to changes in society, the welfare state has taken over part of this role. The humped shape of the age-dependent net contributions captures the essence of the social contract. The pattern displayed in Figure 4.3 is also seen for other countries – and it is hard to think of a tax-financed system without this property. However, in countries with more extended welfare arrangements – like the Nordics – the amplitude is larger; the average person receives more when young and old and contributes more when middle-aged. In countries with a less extended welfare state, less public money is spent on childcare, education, health, and old-age pension, but taxes are also lower. Therefore, the net contributions vary less with age, and the social contract is leaner.

* The net contribution is in thousand Danish kroner defined as tax payments less transfers and individualized services received for an average person at given ages. Non-individualized expenditures are distributed equally over all age groups. Data applies to 2014 for Denmark

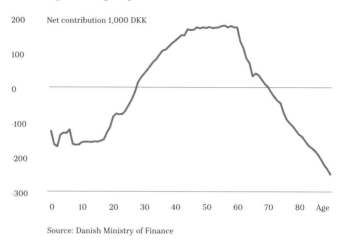

Figure 4.3 Age-dependent net contributions. Denmark, 2014 *

Source: Danish Ministry of Finance

The intergenerational contract is basically a pay-as-you-go arrangement where the tax contributions received in a given year should cover the expenses in a given year. Concretely, the tax payments made by the current middle-aged population cover the net expenses on the current young and old population. The alternating roles over the average person's life cycle, of benefiting from and contributing to the system, are thus consistent with the system being continuously in financial balance.

There are two important points to add to the preceding discussion. First, the public budget does not have to balance period-by-period. Deficits in some periods are allowed, provided there are surpluses in other periods. The automatic stabilizers discussed in Chapter 3 only work if such temporary budget imbalances are possible. Second, looking at Figure 4.3 for Denmark, one may fairly question whether this is consistent with viable public finances, given the discrepancy between the areas above and below the x axis. Merely comparing these areas leads to a hasty conclusion, and mortality must be considered: Not everyone who reaches the age of 40 will reach the age of 80. Taking this into account, the social contract is in financial balance for Denmark and Sweden[8].

The social contract can be interpreted as consisting of two parts. To see this, think of, say, age 40 as a dividing line. In the first phase of life (up to the age of 40), the average person receives childcare and education, and then enters the labor market and pays taxes.

Implicitly, one might think of these taxes as a repayment of what was received in childhood and youth. This is like a borrowing contract: If education is financed by a private loan, the loan has to be paid back upon completion of one's education. In the Nordic welfare model, education is provided for free, but it is implicitly paid back through taxes. It is implicit because the young people receiving education are not contractually obligated to pay back the cost of it, but they do so via tax payments levied on the income they later earn based on their education. The repayment also has an insurance effect, since it is dependent on the outcome of their education, in terms of their later earnings.

Next, consider what happens in the second phase of life (after the age of 40). The average person continues paying taxes, and then later receives a pension, health services, and old-age care. This is like a savings arrangement: You pay first and receive later. Again, it is an implicit contract.

In sum, the social or intergenerational contract has a borrowing or forward-looking part, and a savings or backward-looking part. Here, "forward-looking" means that something is received before contributing, and the inverse is the case for the "backward-looking" aspect. This structure is essential for the influence of the social contract on economic performance and welfare.

The intergenerational contract is quite powerful. Consider the financing of education. Private financing is difficult for a number of reasons. The outcome of edu-

8.
Norway and Finland do not satisfy the conditions for fiscal sustainability, and therefore the issue is more complicated for these countries

9.
The repayment of the loan depends on the future value of the acquired "human capital." But human capital cannot be provided as collateral for a loan, like real capital or tangible assets can. Collateral works to make lending less risky. If the borrower is unable to repay the loan, the lender can seize the collateral and sell it to recover part of the loan. This is obviously not possible for human capital (ruling out slavery), and therefore borrowing based on human capital is difficult

cation is uncertain, and it is difficult to put up collateral for an education loan. Across all countries, private loan financing is a challenge[9]. It is easiest to see the potential of the intergenerational contract by looking at extremes. Consider a case where borrowing is not possible at all, so that education financing is dependent on the willingness and ability of parents to finance education. In this case, not all children will get an education, as some will have parents who are unwilling or unable to pay for their education. While this is extreme, the difference is seen in a comparison between the Nordic countries and the US, for instance, where the financing of college education is a severe challenge for many families, whereas such educations are tax-financed and thus tuition-free in the Nordic countries.

Now, introduce the intergenerational contract and let the public sector offer education to all children and young people, and let it be financed by a tax on the middle-aged (the forward-looking part of the contract). Importantly, this produces a more level playing field (equality of opportunities), improving the scope for all young people, depending on their abilities and motivation to acquire an education. This improves human capital in the economy, increases average income, and contributes to a more equal distribution of income; in short, it creates a situation like the one shown in Figure 4.3.

However, what about the financing of education falling on the shoulders of the middle-aged? They did not get any education, but they are required to pay taxes. Under the social contract, they can be offered a pension when they become old (they cannot save as much as they otherwise would, due to tax payments, but instead they receive a pension). This pension will be paid by the current younger generation when they reach middle age, and since they have received an education and thus have a higher income, this puts them in a position to pay such taxes. Here, the social contract has effectively replaced the capital market and ensured education for the young. All are better off, and income is higher.

The social contract can go even further than this. While the market mechanisms can handle private gains from education, there are also gains to society more generally (a positive externality). The production of knowledge not only benefits those acquiring the knowledge, but also future generations, who can build on the experience and knowledge of past generations. Individuals do not take such externalities into account in their decision-making, and this causes under-investment in the production of human capital. However, in the design of the social contract, such externalities can be considered. Consequently, the social contract can improve on outcomes even if, for example, the capital market is perfect.

The balance between the forward-looking and backward-looking parts of the social contract is essential. Consider the following thought experiment: Would you prefer (a) to receive 1,000 euros today and pay them back at a given future date (loan), or (b) to pay 1,000 euros today and get them back at a given future date (saving)? If there is a positive interest rate, clearly (a) is preferable to (b). Put differently, the forward-looking part of the contract gives an advantage to the individual (borrowing at a low rate), and the backward-looking part is a drawback (saving with a low return). Now consider how the entire social contract looks to a newborn. Is the forward-looking or the backward-looking part dominant? There is a net gain to the newborn if the expected value of what will be received is larger than the expected value of what will be contributed. It turns out that the net value is positive, and significant. A computation for Denmark[10] shows that the expected present value of the social contract to an average Dane born in 2012 is about 80,000 euros, roughly 5 percent of the average present value of lifetime earnings. This

10.
See Andersen, T. M., & Bhattacharya, J. (2017). The intergenerational welfare state and the rise and fall of pay-as-you-go pensions. *Economic Journal*, 127, 896–923

is the direct effect, not including the gain that comes from education in terms of higher income.

Therefore, the nature of the cradle-to-grave model is not only that it redistributes across the life cycle, and in this way performs a capital market function. This role is important in its own right in ensuring more equal opportunities for education. In addition, the social contract releases gains from investments in the young, beyond what is feasible in private markets. Welfare state arrangements may, in this way, be associated with welfare gains. This helps to explain why countries like the Nordics, with large public sectors, can have high income levels and low inequality: The social contract enhances investment in education and human capital accumulation.

Active and passive redistribution

The relatively low level of income inequality in the Nordic countries is one of the key characteristics highlighted above in Figure 4.1. Inequality in disposable income (market incomes after taxes and transfers) depends on the underlying inequality in market incomes (labor and capital) and the extent of redistribution[11]. A country may thus have low income inequality because there is little inequality in market incomes, or because it redistributes a lot, or both. To address this question, Figure 4.4 shows a simple breakdown, across countries, of differences in inequality in disposable incomes due to inequality in market incomes, and to redistribution. The lower inequality in disposable income in Norway, Denmark, and Sweden is attributable, in a 50-50 split, to lower inequality in market incomes and more redistribution. Although redistribution is important in the Nordic countries, it is equally important that the distribution of market incomes displays comparatively low inequality.

11.
The population structure is also important. For instance, more single-person households tend to increase income inequality

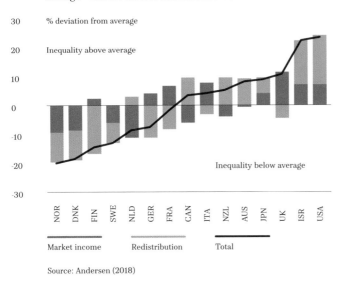

Figure 4.4 Breakdown of difference in inequality from OECD average – market income and redistribution *

Source: Andersen (2018)

* The graph shows how much the Gini coefficient deviates in percent from the OECD average (for countries included in the graph), and breaks this down by inequality in market incomes deviating from the OECD average, and redistribution deviating from the OECD average. Redistribution is measured as the percentage reduction in the Gini coefficient, measured over market and disposable income, respectively. Negative values indicate contribution to lowering inequality below the average, and positive values to raising it above the average. Data applies to 2014

Some countries, like the US, have more inequality in disposable incomes *both* because market incomes are more unequally distributed, *and* because there is less redistribution. Countries like Germany, France, and Italy have inequality in market incomes above the OECD average, but redistribution counteracts the effect on disposable income. In contrast, other countries, like Canada and New Zealand, have less inequality in market incomes, but redistribute less than the average.

This points to an important distinction between active and passive redistribution. The traditional policy discussion focuses on how to repair an unjust distribution of market incomes via taxes and transfers (see Figure 4.1). This is "passive," in the sense that the distribution of market incomes is taken as given, and policies try to modify its consequences. "Active" redistribution attempts to affect the distribution of market incomes via education policies, labor market policies, and so on. More equality can be attained via redistribution, but if the base created by the labor market is not already relatively equal, this has its limits. Ensuring that most people are self-supporting, that is earning a wage that enables a decent living standard, supports equality in the Nordic countries, and their economic performance crucially relies on active policies – again stressing the point that taxes cannot be assessed independently of what they are financing.

This is also important in a forward-looking perspective. Labor markets are affected by new technologies and globalization (see Chapter 7). Without policy initiatives, inequality will grow, and there are limits to how much passive redistribution policies can counteract these trends.

The employment model

One of the striking facts about the Nordic countries is their high employment rates. High taxes and the social safety net might be expected to discourage work. However, employment rates in the Nordic countries are among the highest in the OECD, as illustrated in Figure 4.5. This figure shows the employment rates for different age groups, and therefore also shows employment in a life-cycle profile. For 30-60-year-olds, employment rates in the Nordic countries are among the highest in the OECD. Notably, employment rates for women are almost as high as for men. Equally important is the fact that employment rates are also high for groups with little labor market-relevant education. Note that the inverted U-pattern for employment over the life cycle, shown in Figure 4.5, is the mirror image of the period during which the average person is a net contributor to the welfare state, as shown in Figure 4.3.

Employment rates are relatively low for youth, as seen in Figure 4.5, primarily due to extensive investments in education. The low employment rates for older age groups are attributable to pension schemes and options for early retirement – which are intentional, politically chosen policies, where the classic trade-off is at stake. It should be noted that average working hours per employee are about the average OECD level. Although the high employment rates for both men and women can explain some of this, they are not the whole story.

Figure 4.5 Age dependent employment rates 2019 *

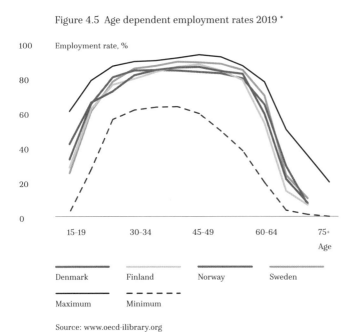

* Employment to population rate for both sexes. "Minimum" is the lowest employment rate for the given age group among OECD countries, and "Maximum" is the highest employment rate for the given age group among OECD countries

Source: www.oecd-ilibrary.org

To explain how high employment rates in the Nordic countries can coexist with high taxes and an extended social safety net, it should be noted that the provision of welfare services may be conducive to employment. The provision of welfare services supports or facilitates labor supply, directly or indirectly, via effects on labor market possibilities (wages). This applies very broadly to education, which improves the qualifications of the labor force, and to health services, which keep the labor force physically and mentally capable of working. It also applies to services that are alternatives to "home-based service provision," like caring for children and the elderly. Public provision of such services lowers the opportunity costs of work. This may be particularly important for the female labor supply, since, for historical reasons, such "home production" has primarily been part of the female domain. Historically, the expansion of the welfare state in the Nordic countries happened simultaneously with the increase in female labor force participation, but clearly the direction of causality can be discussed.

Employment is a core element in the Nordic welfare model, for several reasons. It is essential to maintain a high employment level to ensure an equal distribution of income. The public sector itself is also a large employer and "demander of labor." In the Nordic countries, between a quarter and a third of all employed people work in the public sector. The large supply of welfare services creates a correspondingly large public demand for teachers, nurses, doctors, and so on. A well-functioning labor market is therefore also important from this perspective.

Finally, and crucially, the financial viability of the Nordic welfare model critically depends on maintaining a high employment level. A decline in employment triggers a double budget effect – as it increases expenditures on, for instance, unemployment benefits, and also reduces tax revenue. Since the welfare state is "extended" and very comprehensive, with high benefit levels and high tax rates, it follows that this sensitivity is high (the automatic budget reaction discussed above). For this reason, the public budget is much more sensitive to variations in private employment than in other OECD countries with leaner welfare states. Turning this argument around, this means that if a high employment level cannot be sustained, the financial viability of the model is at stake. No surprise that policy discussions are strongly focused on how to sustain and increase employment rates.

The insights discussed above highlights some of the key economic mechanisms accounting for the performance of the Nordic welfare model. The effects of taxes depend on what type of activities are financed, and in the Nordic countries, repairing market failures and providing insurance are essential elements. This explains why the Nordic countries can reconcile a large public sector with a favorable economic performance and relatively low income inequality. This is not to deny that there is a trade-off between incentives and redistribution/insurance in the design of economic policies; this trade-off is explicitly addressed, for instance by labor market policies and active spending that supports employment and productivity. The following chapters consider, in more detail, some key properties of the Nordic welfare model. As pointed out, the specific policy design differs across the Nordic countries, and therefore the next chapters primarily focus on Denmark as a case in point.

Chapter 5.

Labor markets and the flexicurity model

Key objectives in the Nordic welfare model are tied to labor market performance. For the individual, the ability to be independent and self-supporting depends on employment, income, and work conditions. A high employment rate and decent wages are pivotal, both for living standards and for the distribution of income. Finally, the employment rate is of critical importance for public finances.

Labor markets are in constant flux. The demand for labor varies with the business cycle situation, and structural changes create jobs and destroy jobs. These changes imply both challenges and opportunities for workers. *Ex ante*, the risk of reductions in real income, most markedly in the case of job loss, is crucial and creates a fundamental need for insurance and security. At the same time, it is important that the incentive structure supports flexibility and job searching, such that firms can easily adjust their workforce to changing market conditions. In short, both security and flexibility are important.

Reconciling labor market flexibility and security is a fundamental policy issue, and new technologies and globalization have intensified the discussion about how to strike a balance between the two (Moene 2010; see also Chapter 7). In this context, the Nordic welfare model has been highlighted as an example of how to accomplish "inclusive growth," such that the gains from economic progress do not produce more inequality and fragmentation of population groups. In particular, the concept widely known as "flexicurity," and associated with the Danish labor market, has been drawn into focus, as discussed later in this chapter.

Flexibility and security

Labor market risks cannot be avoided. The crucial question is: Who should carry the consequence of the risks? Risks can be diversified in many different ways. To discuss possible arrangements, consider first a setting where either employers or workers carry the risk. If the employer ends up carrying the risk, workers are offered job/income security either via long periods of notice, or severance pay if they are laid off. However, this imposes a cost on employers, which may be problematic for small employers in particular. If it is difficult or costly for employers to lay off workers, they may be more reluctant to hire in the first place, or prefer to hire based on temporary contracts, as is the case in countries like France and Italy. The latter, temporary option gives the employer more flexibility, but transfers the risk to workers. Leaving all the risk on workers has potentially large welfare costs, since it is difficult to diversify human capital risk in financial markets. There is a fundamental conflict between flexibility for employers and security for workers.

This raises the question of whether there is some scope for collective risk-sharing, such that neither the single employer nor the single worker carries the risk and its potential consequences. An unemployment insurance system financed by contributions (taxes) by employers and workers is an example of a collective risk-sharing arrangement. All contribute, and those unlucky enough to lose their jobs are entitled to an unemployment benefit. No single employer or worker carries the full consequences of the risk. This system therefore has the potential to combine flexibility for employers to hire and fire workers, with security for workers. Such a system protects workers rather than specific jobs, and thus helps to preserve labor market flexibility. Systems of this kind exist in most countries, but their generosity varies considerably. The Nordic countries stand out by offering relatively high compensation to low-income groups.

The Achilles heel of such a system is its implied incentive structure. This applies to employers and workers alike. On the employers' side, there may be excessive lay-offs and insufficient incentives to train workers, since they can easily move to competitors. On the worker side, there is the classic dilemma that a small income loss when becoming unemployed (insurance) implies a low income gain when returning to work (incentives). Adequate income insurance in case of unemployment thus raises an incentive problem, in terms of job searching and "reservation demands" to acceptable jobs. Balancing these opposing effects is a crucial design issue for labor market policies and unemployment insurance systems.

Some additional remarks on risk are in order. The type of risk clearly depends on the employer/industry structure of the economy. Large corporations can more easily accommodate shocks than small businesses, for instance by internally reallocating workers. A country with an industry structure consisting of a few key industries is more vulnerable than a country with industries diversified across sector types. To complicate the picture, these structural characteristics may also change in response to the labor market structures and institutions. A system with collective risk-sharing is more valuable for small businesses facing a volatile market, and vice versa. This points to the fact that policies and institutional structures are also part of the specialization (comparative advantages) of countries, and it explains why there is not one optimal model. Which design is best depends on a multitude of factors.

The following considers, in more detail, how these design issues are addressed in the Danish "flexicurity" model.

The flexicurity model

The Danish model, known as "flexicurity," is often highlighted as a well-functioning labor market that reconciles flexibility for employers and security for workers. High employment rates, low wage dispersion, and low unemployment are among the features often lauded as indicators of a successful labor market.

The development in the Danish labor market is summarized in Figure 5.1, showing the unemployment rate in comparison to the OECD average. While the unemployment rate in recent years – including during the financial crisis starting in 2008 and the ongoing COVID-19 crisis – has been below the OECD level, this has only applied since the early 1990s. Prior to that, unemployment rates were persistently high.

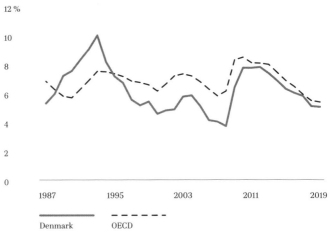

Figure 5.1 Unemployment rate in Denmark and OECD, 1991–2019

Denmark   OECD

Source: www.oecd-ilibrary.org

The short version of the Danish flexicurity model is that hiring and firing rules are rather flexible, and unemployment insurance is generous by international standards. However, this was also the case in the period from the mid-1970s to the early 1990s, when the Danish labor market did not perform well. Therefore, the flexibility and the security part of the Danish policy package cannot, in isolation, account for labor market performance in more recent times. This point does not deny the importance of these elements, but it does emphasize that they are no guarantee of a low and stable unemployment rate.

The pivotal change came with a series of reforms during the latter half of the 1990s. After the reforms, Denmark shifted from having an unemployment rate systematically above the OECD average, to performing consistently better (see Figure 5.1). The main thrust of these reforms[12] was a shift from a passive focus on income protection to a more active focus on job searching and employment. The policy tightened eligibility for unemployment benefits and

12.
See, e.g., Andersen, T. M., & Svarer, M. (2007). Flexicurity: Labour Market Performance in Denmark. *CESifo Economic Studies, 53(3)*, 389–429

shortened their duration, in several steps, from seven to four years, and it also introduced workfare elements into unemployment insurance and social policies in general. Workfare or active labor market policies include activity conditionalities – like active job searching, participation in educational programs, or job training – as part of the eligibility rules for unemployment benefits and "social assistance" of the type mentioned in Chapter 3. The workfare policies had the dual purpose of strengthening the incentive structure for people to search for and accept jobs, and to improve the qualifications of the unemployed to enhance their job-finding prospects.

The "flex" part of the flexicurity concept refers to lenient employment protection, making it relatively easy for employers to adjust their workforce. The "[se]curity" part captures the generous income support for the unemployed. Flexicurity can thus be said to be a misnomer, since the two aspects, in themselves, did not produce very good outcomes. The favorable performance of the Danish labor market critically relies on active labor market policies to counteract the possible disincentive effects of generous income support to the unemployed while maintaining the insurance aspect.

Turning to the details of the security element, unemployment insurance in Denmark is voluntary and financed partly by membership contributions and partly by the state, and therefore taxes. Unemployed people who are not entitled to unemployment benefits have access to "social assistance," a benefit where the level is generally lower, and which is means-tested against family income.

For work-related injuries (other health problems are covered by the public sector), maternity leave, and training, collective or pooling programs exist and are part of the collective agreements made between the "social partners." Employers contribute to the programs, and expenses are financed out of a common pool. These arrangements are constructed to provide both insurance and incentives via collective programs. Take training – compensating firms' wage expenditure when apprentices and trainees attend college or training programs, and internships – as an example. All employers have an interest in young people getting a proper professional education and training to create a pool of well-qualified workers from which they can recruit. For a single employer, investing in training is costly and risky, since a trained person can easily move to another employer, and hence the investment is lost. This problem is larger when labor flexibility is high. Obviously, this reduces the incentive to invest in such training, and may encourage employers to free-ride on the training investments made by other employers. All employers reason in this way, and the level of training becomes sub-optimally low, to the disadvantage of the entire business community, workers, and society. To overcome these problems, Denmark has a program to which all private employers contribute, and those that take apprentices get a subsidy from the common pool. There are similar arrangements for maternity leave and work-related injuries.

These arrangements underline several points. First, they show that labor market organizations play a critical role, and key risk-sharing and collective arrangements are not only supplied by the state. Moreover, by establishing programs where basic security items like unemployment benefits, healthcare, maternity leave, pensions, and so on are not tied to a specific employer, security is maintained without hampering labor market flexibility. The broad coverage is serving political objectives and contributing to a well-functioning labor market. Finally, there is a chicken-and-egg issue: Should these programs be seen as a response to the particular structure in the country (Denmark has many small businesses), or is it the other way around – that these structures have called for such arrangements?

Labor market performance

Details of institutions, rules, and regulations are complex, and it is therefore difficult to compare and classify countries, not least in quantitative terms, using a few summary indicators. Within the OECD, Denmark has one of the most generous unemployment insurance systems, measured by the net replacement rate in the first year of unemployment, and spends most on active labor market policies (OECD 2019). Measuring labor market flexibility by the OECD index for employment protection legislation, it is about average, but using other more performance-related measures, flexibility is high (see below). In the World Economic Forum's competitiveness assessment, based on a 2018 survey of business leaders, Denmark has the fourth most flexible labor market, out of 141 countries.

Rather than a list of institutional details, the salient features can be illustrated by considering how the Danish flexicurity model coped with the financial crisis. It may be argued that a system is only really tested in a crisis. While the model is no guarantee against business cycle fluctuations, the interesting question is how it performs under a severe recession. Lenient firing rules make it likely that employment will fall drastically when aggregate demand drops, and although the social safety net cushions incomes for the unemployed, the financial viability of the Danish welfare model is at risk if employment permanently decreases (see Chapter 4). A prolonged decline in employment reduces tax revenues and increases social expenditures, and thus puts public finances under strain.

Denmark was very severely hit by the financial crisis. Measured by GDP, the economy shrank by 5 percent between 2008 and 2009 – among the largest declines in the OECD. The period prior to what is now also known as "the Great Recession" had high growth, and unemployment fell below the structural level. There were clear signs of overheating, with a booming housing market and accelerating wage increases. This was an unsustainable situation, and economic growth was already fading when the Great Recession set in and brought the economy into a deep recession. These developments had huge labor market impacts. Prior to the Great Recession, the employment rate was at a record high, but then it plummeted rapidly, and the recovery was slow. The Danish labor market was harder hit and recovered more slowly than in many other countries. Unemployment increased by 2.5 percentage points between 2008 and 2009, and by 4 percentage points between 2008 and 2010, almost double the increase for OECD countries on average, although unemployment remained below the OECD average (see Figure 5.1). The unemployment rate has since declined, and employment rates have reached the levels that prevailed before the crisis. At the moment of writing, it is too early to conclude on the impacts of the COVID-19 crisis, but the overall dynamism and adjustment capability seems to be intact.

A key property of the flexicurity model is a high level of job turnover, implying that the unemployed (and also the young people entering the labor market) can find a job fairly easily, and that most unemployment spells are short. The general level of job inflows and outflows is high. Although job inflows plummeted as a consequence of the financial crisis, they soon recovered, and the gross inflow and outflow rates quickly returned to the levels seen before the crisis.

Across time, dynamics have been substantially. Approximately 1 in 5 jobs in the private sector existing at the start of a year have disappeared at the start of the next year. The rate of job destruction is high; luckily the rate of job creation is at the same high level. Underneath relatively steady employment rates, there is thus a very high rate of turnover; the labor market is very dynamic. This is a key characteristic of the flexicurity labor market.

This has several important implications. One is that most unemployment spells are short: While the risk of losing one's job is relatively high, the chances of finding a new one are equally high. The turnover rates are high from a comparative perspective, and the transition rate from unemployment into employment is also high (see Figure 5.2). The high level of flexibility is of great value to employers, and workers are not too severely affected. Interestingly, in a 2017 survey, 82 percent of Danish respondents said that they consider their current job situation to be "very good" or "rather good" – the highest among the then 28 EU countries.[13]

13.
See http://ec.europa.eu/ commfront-office/ publicopin-ion/ index.cfm/ Chart getChart/ theme-Ky/27/group-Ky/167

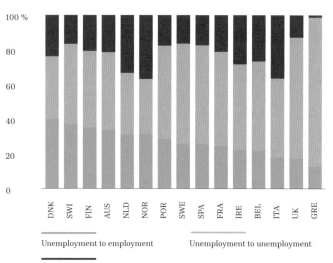

Figure 5.2 Labor market transitions for the unemployed, selected European countries, 2019 *

Unemployment to employment   Unemployment to unemployment

Unemployment to inactivity

Source: http://ec.europa.eu/eurostat

* The transition rate between given labor market status is shown quarter-to-quarter, here from unemployment to employment, unemployment, or inactivity. Data is not seasonally adjusted. Average transition rates for 2019, second quarter (Q2). Only selected EU countries are shown. Denmark has the highest transition rate from unemployment to employment among all EU countries

It is also a consequence of the high level of turnover in the labor market that youth and long-term unemployment are low in international comparisons. High turnover rates thus effectively work as an implicit work-sharing mechanism. Equal burden-sharing is important from a distributional perspective, but it is also of structural importance. The alternative would be longer unemployment spells concentrated on a smaller group of individuals, more long-term unemployed, and a corresponding depreciation of human and social capital. In short, the high turnover rates reduce the negative structural implications of high unemployment.

Labor market policies

High minimum wages are a potential barrier to finding a job. If a certain worker is not worth the minimum wage, no employer will hire that worker. Therefore, it is essential to ensure that most people enter the labor market with qualifications that make them at least worth the minimum wage to an employer. Educational policies, and also the active labor market policies, are particularly important in this respect (see Chapter 4).

"Activation policies" are an integral part of the Danish labor market model. Workfare policies of this type, which are intended to activate job-seekers, have been continuously revised and adjusted in light of experience, research, and policy discussions. Most recently, the focus has been two-fold. First, for young people, the system has a strong focus on ensuring that all young people obtain a labor market-relevant education. This is reflected in a recent reform of the "social assistance" system. For individuals below the age of 30 (previously, the critical age was 25) without a qualifying education, the social assistance level has been reduced, such that it does not provide better compensation than the standard Danish study grants. Eligibility for support requires commencement of education;

alternatively, participation in an "activation program" is mandatory.

Second, activation policies have been changed from a rather rigid, programmatic range of interventions to a more flexible system directed towards labor market needs and with a more individual focus, relying more on job-searching and skill-matching than program participation, as well as incentives to ensure a quicker return to employment. In the first part of an unemployment spell (3 months for people under 30, 6 months for people aged 30–49, and 3 months for people over 50), the main intervention takes the form of meetings and counselling. The aim is to strengthen and target job-search activities. Further into the unemployment spell comes program participation (as a right and duty). In addition, all unemployed people have the right to participate in an education program lasting up to six weeks (individually chosen from a shortlist). The pendulum is thus swinging away from very rigid activation policies towards more flexible policies, and since the policy shift is still under implementation, it is too early to assess how it is working.

Chapter 6.

Aging populations

Pension reforms are at the top of the economic-political agendas in the Nordic countries, as well as in many other countries. Populations are aging, due partly to declining fertility rates and partly to increasing longevity; in short, there are fewer children and young people, and more old people. Increases in longevity are driven by lower mortality at higher ages, and these increases are significant and associated with substantial welfare gains – even while raising questions about the adequacy and financing of pensions. Pension systems are already suffering from either inadequacy or funding problems in many countries, and in a forward-looking perspective these problems will be magnified by demographic developments.

The demographic challenge can be illustrated by considering a measure called the "dependency ratio," giving the number of individuals above age 65 in the population relative to the number of individuals aged 15-64. This is a rough measure of how many old people need to be supported, relative to the number in the working-age group able to provide or finance this support. According to the United Nations population forecast,[14] the old-age dependency ratio for high-income countries is going to increase from 30.9% in 2020 to 54.2% in 2060, and still further

14.
See https://esa.
un.org/ unpd/wpp/,
the medium variant
forecast

after that. The Nordic countries are facing similar developments; in DK, from 34.9% to 47.2%; in Finland, from 40.1% to 56.3%; in Norway, from 29.6% to 47.1%; and in Sweden, from 35.9% to 51.5%.

Aging populations are raising difficult political questions. Providing decent pensions, health services, and old-age care is a key policy objective in all countries. In some countries, pension systems are not well developed, and in others the aging population will create substantial financial problems. The OECD (2019) predicts that expenditures on pensions will increase from the current figure of about 9 percent of GDP to 11 percent of GDP in 2060. On top of this come expenditures on health and old-age care. For most countries, the expenditure path is a mirror of the development in the dependency ratio, which is a gradual but steady upward expenditure drift where healthcare is as important a driver as pensions. Aging is a particular challenge for the Nordic model, due to the "extended social contract" and the importance of healthcare and pensions, as discussed in Chapter 4.

Pension systems

The pension system has multiple objectives, which can be split into three main categories. There is a distributional concern to ensure that all elderly people have a decent living standard (minimum standards). It is also important to ensure that living standards after retirement stand in a reasonable relation to living standards while working. Finally, there are insurance aspects to ensure coverage of various eventualities, including a long life (life annuities) and the needs of a surviving spouse and children.

Given these multiple objectives, there is not one unique optimal pension system. The most adequate design depends on the weighting of these different objectives. This does not imply, however, that the design of the pension system does not matter. Quite the contrary; the design of the pension system is crucial, and it is important to be explicit about the pros and cons of the different design elements and how they relate to the various objectives the system must achieve.

Pension systems are characterized by their membership group, contributions, mode of financing, and benefit structure for the retired, to mention only a few general features. Accordingly, they have many dimensions and can be designed in many different ways, as is also seen from the cross-country variations[15].

One key dimension of pension systems is their funding, for which there are two basic systems. One is a "pay-as-you-go" system (PAYG) where benefits to current pensioners are financed by contributions/taxes levied on the current labor force. The other is a fully funded (FF) system where individuals contribute (defined contributions) to a pension fund during their working lives, and the contributions plus the market return on their investments determine what pension the given individual is entitled to when retired. These two systems have various pros and cons.

It is an important theoretical insight, and empirical fact, that an FF system offers a higher rate of return to pension contributions than a PAYG system. If one's only concern is to find the pension system yielding the highest return, the balance tips in favor of an FF system. However, there are many other concerns. The first is that implementing an FF system takes a long time, since people have to save throughout their entire working lives to accumulate funds for their pension. A PAYG system has the advantage that it can immediately provide pensions to the elderly, financed by the working-age population (as part of the "social contract" discussed in Chapter 4). Moreover, an FF system projects work-life income into a pension and can therefore be said to reproduce the distribution profile of income, which ensures that pensions are in propor-

15.
The OECD publication *Pensions at a glance* (2019) provides an overview of pension systems in OECD countries

tion to the wage earned (replacement rates), but takes no distributional considerations. As a result, there is general agreement that some PAYG pensions are needed for distributional reasons. The different types of pension systems therefore have different purposes, which is why actual pension plans typically include an element of both. However, pension system designs vary considerably across countries.

Pension systems are a case in point, showing that although the Nordic countries share many similarities, their specific policy and institutional settings differ. In Denmark, the system is organized around "funded occupational pension schemes" along with PAYG public pensions, while Sweden has adopted a "notionally defined pension scheme" that is largely a PAYG-based system in which pensions stand in relation to labor income earned during the working years. Norway and Finland have pension systems that fall between these two types of pension systems.

The Nordic countries – especially Denmark and Sweden – have been front-runners in undertaking reforms to maintain the financial viability of welfare and pension systems when the dependency ratio increases. Major changes in the pension systems of both countries were carried out in the early 1990s. Although different routes were taken, the aim was to ensure decent living standards for all elderly people (distribution), and to have pensions that are reasonable when compared to incomes while working (consumption smoothing). More recently, the focus has shifted more to ensuring incentives for working seniors to postpone retirement when longevity increases.

These relatively early reform initiatives pay off today, since Denmark and Sweden are among the few countries that are not facing a fiscal sustainability problem due to aging while, at the same time, their populations can look forward to decent pensions. Since there are many institutional details, the following section focuses on the

Danish pension system as an example of how to ensure a robust pension system capable of coping with an aging population.

The Danish pension system

The Danish pension system is consistently ranked at the very top of the Melbourne Mercer Global Pension Index[16] as having "A first class and robust retirement income system that delivers good benefits, is sustainable and has a high level of integrity." While many details of such rankings can be discussed and contested, this assessment at least shows that the Danish pension system has some degree of merit.

The Danish system is a hybrid in which both public (PAYG) and private pensions (FF) play important roles. The basic structure is as follows: The public pension includes a basic amount (flat-rate pension) for all[17], and means-tested supplements. Furthermore, there are a number of age-dependent supplements. These pension entitlements are of the "defined benefit" type and are tax-financed. Public pensions are indexed to wages.

By law, all wage earners and recipients of transfer income contribute to the "supplementary labor market pension" (ATP, in Danish). This is a defined contribution plan to which everyone in the above groups contributes the same monthly amount (depending on working hours). The ATP is a life annuity that contributes to maintaining a decent living standard for all elderly people.

"Labor market pensions" are agreed upon as part of an employment relationship or through collective agreements negotiated between the "social partners." The development of labor market pensions gained momentum in the late 1980s, and subsequently the arrangements have been extended to cover a large part of the labor market; contribution rates were increasing until recently. Labor market pensions are individual and portable across differ-

16.
See https://info.mercer.com/

17.
To get the full amount, there is a requirement that the individual has lived in Denmark for at least 40 years from the age of 15. If the residence period is shorter, the pension is reduced proportionally

ent types of jobs. The pension benefit typically includes life annuities and benefits paid over a fixed period of time (rate pension).

Today, contribution rates vary between 12 and 18 percent, with rates tending to be higher for high-income groups. It takes a long time to phase in such a system, and not until 2040–2050 will individuals be able to retire after having saved at current contribution rates throughout their entire working lives.

Private pension savings comprise other forms of savings (voluntary savings), as well as savings in pension arrangements with banks and insurance companies (where the return is taxed more leniently, but the funds are tied to retirement).

The various elements of the Danish pension system serve several purposes. The public pension and ATP constitute the base of the system, providing the minimum income that all pensioners are assured, independently of any labor market pension or other private savings. Public pension supplements are means-tested against income and wealth, targeting economically disadvantaged pensioners. This serves the distributional objective. Labor market pensions depend on the extent of work and income during a person's economically active years, as well as the return on the accumulated funds. High employment rates and income result in high contributions and thus high pension savings, and in turn higher consumption opportunities as a pensioner. Labor market pensions therefore play a decisive role in ensuring that the consumption opportunities of pensioners stand in relation to their situation prior to retirement (consumption smoothing). Finally, voluntary private pension savings give individuals the opportunity to add to their pensions.

Figure 6.1 shows replacement rates, that is, pensions relative to income prior to retirement, across the income distribution, capturing the essence of the Danish system. This also shows the role of the different elements in the pension system.

First, replacement rates close to 100 percent for low-income groups (1st decile) reflect that social transfers for non-employed working-age people are close to the full public pension (base pension plus supplements). Most people with income in the 1st decile are out of work and receive a social transfer. Hence, the replacement rate is close to 100 percent, and poverty among the elderly is rare. The level of public pensions is such that very few elderly (in 2017: 0.3 percent) end up in the low-income group with a disposable income below 50 percent of the median income. Those in low-income groups are often immigrants who do not meet the full residence requirement for the public pensions.

Second, the replacement rate for high-income groups (5th decile or above) is about 65 percent. This is high in comparison to other OECD countries (OECD 2019), and shows that the pension system ensures consumption smoothing.

Third, the composition of the replacement ratio shows the division of labor between the different elements in the pension system. Since public pensions are targeting the distributional objective, their relative role is declining, while the relative role of private pensions is increasing in the income level. This is an intended implication of the means-testing of supplements in the public pension system. Looking ahead, this will become even more pronounced, since private pensions are still in a transition phase. Replacement rates will increase, and private pensions will increase in importance, although public pensions will retain their distributional role.

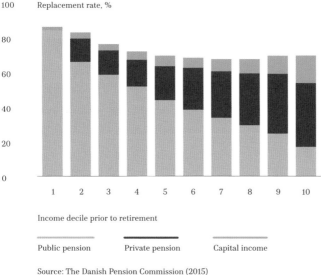

Figure 6.1 Average replacement rates in Denmark at age 66 across income deciles *

Replacement rate, %

Income decile prior to retirement

Public pension   Private pension   Capital income

Source: The Danish Pension Commission (2015)

* Replacement rates are computed for individual disposable income at age 66, relative to the disposable income at age 55–57 (also the incomes used for the construction of income deciles). The disposable income at age 55–57 is adjusted to the 2014 level by use of the index for general wage development

Means-testing of public pensions (supplements) serves the targeting purpose of ensuring that all pensioners have a decent living standard. However, it also implies that increased private savings, and thus private pensions, are not reflected one-to-one in the total pensions. Over a certain income interval, increasing private pension savings reduces supplements. Means-testing therefore effectively entails an implicit tax on private savings. In considering the incentives to save and retire, one must consider not only formal taxes but also the implicit taxes arising via means-testing. The implicit tax rates can be rather high, especially for low- to medium-income groups, creating disincentives for pension saving and postponing retirement. This is a classic policy dilemma. The implicit tax rates could be reduced by giving the supplements to all, but this would be very expensive, and the implied tax increases would add to the standard tax distortions.

A further challenge for the Danish pension system is that not everyone is covered by a mandatory labor market pension. Groups left uncovered include employees who fall outside the bargaining areas covered by pensions, as well as self-employed people and individuals with a more marginal attachment to the labor market. Since the system builds on the combination of public pensions and mandatory occupational pensions, this "residual group" falls between the cracks in the system.

Retirement ages

The statutory retirement or pension age is a crucial factor. The lower the retirement age, the higher the savings/contribution rate has to be, or the lower the pension benefit. This applies to both a PAYG and an FF pension system. This choice comes to the fore because of the significant increases in longevity. While an average person at the age of 60 in a high-income country[18] today has an expected remaining lifetime of 24.8 years, this will increase to 28.5 years by 2060-65. For Denmark, the corresponding numbers increase from 23.9 to almost 28 years; for Finland, from 25.1 to 28.9 years; for Norway, from 25.1 to 28.5 years; and for Sweden, from 25.3 to 29.1 years.

If longevity is increasing and pension ages stay unchanged, the retirement period increases. Who is going to finance this? In a PAYG scheme, it will be the current taxpayers. Is it reasonable that they should pay higher taxes to finance a longer retirement period? The social contract discussed in Chapter 4 requires a balance between the number of years the average person contributes to the system and the number of years they benefit from the system. The implication is that if longevity is increasing, pension ages should increase too.

Many countries have discussed such increases in pension ages, and a number have taken steps in that direction, including the Nordics. This is also the case in

18.
See https://esa.
un.org/unpd/wpp/,
the medium variant
forecast

Denmark, where statutory ages in the pension system (for public pensions and for early retirement, along with age limits for payment of funds from pension plans) are established by legislation and thus regulated at a political level. Recent Danish reforms – the welfare reform of 2006, and the retirement reform of 2011 – have raised these ages considerably to cope with an aging population.

These reforms have two elements. The first is a raising of the retirement/pension age, from 65 to 67 years, to catch up with increases in longevity. The second is an indexation of the retirement age to the development in life expectancy at the age of 60, in order to target an expected pension period of 14½ years (17½ including early retirement) in the long run. Currently, the expected retirement period is about 18½ years (23½ years including early retirement). The indexation aims to ensure that the retirement age is tied to longevity, and avoiding that future pensions age depends on current forecasts of longevity.

Increasing the retirement age in step with increases in longevity makes sense in the presence of so-called healthy aging, which adds more healthy years to life, and therefore represents the potential for people to stay on longer in the labor market. This is an "average" argument: While the average person experiences healthy aging, this is not the case for all those who grow old. This raises the difficult question of how to design a system such that those capable of working continue to do so, while those with reduced work capability are allowed to retire early. If a person suffers from severe problems that make it difficult to continue working, the problem is straightforward, and a disability pension can be granted. The difficult cases are the intermediate situations where a person's work capability is severely reduced, but not enough to qualify for a disability pension. The policy dilemma is that if the criteria for disability pension are too lenient, too many people may opt out of the labor market early. If the criteria are too restrictive, it harms those who have serious difficulties in continuing to work. This is an important policy issue that does not have a perfect solution, although potential solutions are currently the topic of intense political debate.

The Danish pension system is one example of how welfare arrangements have been changed to address important challenges. The solution can be described as "semi-privatization," due to the large role of the funded labor market pensions. It is market-based in the sense of being a funded system, but social concerns have also been addressed by making it mandatory. In this way, key welfare state objectives are maintained, and since this relieves the public budget (and thus taxes) from a financing burden, it may even be said that the possibilities of meeting them have been improved.

Chapter 7.

Globalization and migration

An ongoing globalization process allows countries to further divide labor and exploit economies of scale between countries, which in turn is a potential source of further growth. Globalization is widely perceived to be a particular threat to tax-financed welfare states, since high taxes and social standards are challenged by global market forces. The Nordic model was not developed under a shield that protected against international integration – quite the contrary; tight international integration was one of the premises. Hence, the globalization challenge is not new per se, but it may intensify and take on new forms (Andersen et al. 2007). This fuels a debate about whether it is becoming more difficult to maintain "extended welfare states" in the light of ongoing globalization processes.

"Globalization" is a broad term capturing a multitude of factors that affect society at large. A common denominator is that information, capital (financial and real), goods, and (some) services can be more easily exchanged across countries, and likewise the scope for migration/ mobility of people across countries widens. The process is driven both by political decisions to integrate (tariff reductions, trade agreements, EU, and so on) and by technological changes that reduce information and transportation costs. The consequences are potentially wide-ranging, from cultural influences via information exchange and media influence, to distinctly economic implications, including growth in trade and foreign direct investments.

One concern is whether globalization at the start of the twenty-first century poses a particular threat to welfare systems compared to past experiences, particularly that production is becoming more footloose, as reflected in increasing production relocation (outsourcing), at the same time as financial capital, in particular, is becoming nationless. Another concern is whether the global economy can absorb the entry of large players like China and India without undergoing significant restructuring, which in turn challenges the established position of the "old" countries, especially the OECD countries.

It is commonly agreed that economic integration is associated with gains from trade, making it possible to improve living standards. Crucially, these gains can only be reaped through structural changes. The gains from trade arise by aligning production to comparative advantages; that is, in order to harvest the gains, some domestic production activities have to be scaled down or closed, while others expand. These structural changes create both losers and winners across employers, workers, and geographical areas.

The labor market consequences are crucial for how globalization affects income distribution. A relocation of production is also a relocation of jobs. Such change – or even the mere threat of it – affects labor markets: Some people will experience deteriorating wage and job prospects, some will experience improvements, and some will find their future position more uncertain. These threats and opportunities are not uniformly distributed, and therefore inequality tends to increase. There has been a lively discussion as to whether the main driver is technological change or globalization. In many cases, it is hard to separate these two trends, and for the present discussion, the distinction is not crucial.

There have been recurrent discussions about the sustainability of the Nordic model, with alternating waves of optimism and pessimism. In some periods, the near-death of the model has been predicted. In others, the model is heralded for its performance and held up as an example to be followed by others. This is also seen in the current discussion, which features some views on the difficulty of maintaining extended welfare states in a more globalized world, and other views that believe the model exemplifies how to maintain social cohesion in a rapidly changing environment (Ocampo & Stiglitz 2018).

The Nordic welfare model and globalization

The debate on the scope for maintaining and developing the extended the Nordic welfare model in a more globalized era features three main lines of reasoning.

The "race to the bottom" or "systems competition" view holds that fiercer competition between countries follows when it is easier to relocate economic activities across countries (Sinn 2003). Countries endeavor to remain competitive, which inevitably leads to a process of undercutting each other in terms of taxes, social protection, and so on. This will in turn erode the financial basis for an extended welfare model and lead to convergence towards a lean (minimum) public sector.

Another viewpoint argues that welfare states as seen in the Nordic countries were developed in response not only to various changes in society, including different family structures and gender equalization, but also to risks and structural changes induced by international integration. One argument is that it is necessary to expand welfare arrangements to compensate potential losers, to ensure political support for further integration. Moreover, globalization leads to more volatility and risk, which in turn increases the need for insurance arrangements of the type offered by the welfare state. Therefore, the welfare state will expand in response to globalization. This viewpoint thus predicts a growth in welfare arrangements and therefore some convergence to more extended welfare models.

A third view that contests both types of convergence in welfare state policies – in either a downward or an upward direction[19] – is the "new politics of the welfare state." This view argues that there is very strong institutional inertia causing path dependence, which explains why there is no convergence to one welfare model, as discussed in relation to the data reported in Chapter 2. Changing the status quo is difficult, due to the power of various interest groups, and therefore most policy reforms are incremental (parametric rather than structural). As a consequence, differences in welfare regimes persist across countries.

It is useful to consider the development in the overall size of the public sector, since this is at the core of the convergence discussion. The extent of welfare arrangements measured by public sector size displays strong persistence across OECD countries. Figure 7.1 shows the size of the public sector in the mid-1980s and the 2010s measured by the tax burden; that is, total tax revenue as a share of GDP (a similar relation applies to total expenditures as a share of GDP). Strong persistence prevails: Countries with a relatively lean public sector in the 1980s also have a lean public sector in the 2010s, and vice versa (see also Figure 3.1). This shows that various hypotheses on trend changes in the public sector do not hold true for OECD countries over this period. It also shows that quite different social or welfare systems co-exist within the OECD.

19.
See, e.g., Pierson, P. (2001). *The New Politics of the Welfare State*. Cambridge University Press

* The size of the public sector measured by the total tax burden. Five-year averages are shown to reduce the importance of cyclical variations. The line is the 45-degree line corresponding to unchanged public sector size

Figure 7.1 Public sector size in the 1980s and 2010s, OECD countries *

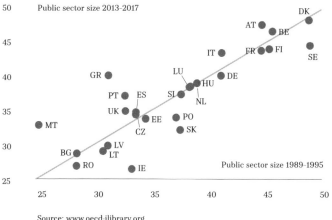

Source: www.oecd-ilibrary.org

This leaves a static impression of the welfare state, as if there have been no changes: a stalemate caused by political or other factors. This is not the case, for several reasons.

There are areas where the race-to-the bottom mechanism is evident. A notable case is corporate taxation. For OECD countries there has been a trend decline in the corporate tax rate, from an average rate close to 50 percent in 1995 to about 22 percent in 2019 – a process clearly driven by countries being concerned about taxing corporations at higher rates than competing countries. However, it is noteworthy that the revenue from corporate taxation has been fairly constant, at a level of about 2.5 percent of GDP over this period. In other words, there is no trend decline in revenue, suggesting that, so far, corporate tax competition has not undermined the financial viability of public sectors. This is not to deny that tax rate reductions matter, though, since revenue could have been higher; however, it also depends on profit developments, the shifting of income between the personal and the corporate tax base,

85

and other effects. These developments are also a reminder that corporate taxation is not a major financing source for the Nordic welfare model (see Chapter 3).

The fact that the overall size of the public sector has been relatively stable across OECD countries cannot be taken as evidence that welfare states are static (Andersen & Molander 2003). It is more a reflection of the fact that solutions are sought within the framework of existing welfare arrangements. The overriding objectives have not changed, but the way of reaching them may have been affected by technological changes, globalization, and so on. What can be inferred from the data is that historically it has not been impossible to maintain a large public sector, even for very open economies.

The discussion about welfare states and globalization, and in particular the convergence towards a leaner welfare model, often makes analogies with firms that are competing to survive. This analogy is misleading for several reasons. First, even private firms competing in the same market can exhibit substantial differences in organization, culture, and strategies. Second, competition is not one-dimensional, but includes many aspects. Basic trade theory teaches us that comparative and not absolute advantages matter, and it is useful to call this lesson to mind in the present context. "Being competitive" is not tantamount to "being alike" and implying that all welfare models have to converge. It is not clear that one model is superior. They all have advantages and disadvantages – especially as they relate to private sector activities, labor markets, and so on.

Countries with flexible employment protection legislation and generous unemployment insurance, like Denmark, may have a comparative advantage in industries with substantial short-term variation in demand and thus in production, while countries with stricter employment protection legislation and less generous unemployment insurance may have a comparative advantage in the production of commodities with less variability. Empirical work[20] finds that countries with more flexible labor markets have a higher degree of specialization in sectors more frequently exposed to sector-specific shocks. This may be interpreted in the sense that the nature of shocks or the need for adjustment is, to some extent, endogenous, meaning that countries (or rather, their companies in the private sector) specialize in the activities for which their particular institutional setting has a comparative advantage. This tends to create persistence in institutions. The important lesson – repeating basic insights from trade theory – is that competitiveness is a question of comparative advantages (see Chapter 5), and that different welfare models may have different comparative advantages.

20.
See Cuñat, A., & Melitz, M. (2012). Volatility, labor market flexibility, and the pattern of comparative advantage. *Journal of the European Economic Association, 10(2),* 225-254

Migration

The increased mobility of goods, services, and capital is qualitatively different from the mobility of people. The mobility and migration of people is a particular challenge to the Nordic welfare model. The "magnet hypothesis" argues that generous welfare states face an asymmetric migration pattern, since they attract migrants who will benefit from the welfare system, and deter potential net contributors. More concretely, generous welfare states are more attractive to migrants without an education, since they benefit from the welfare state and would have difficulties coping in countries with more liberal welfare states, and vice versa. If there is such a pattern in migration flows, it is clearly going to affect the financial balance of the welfare state.

There is a huge migration pressure from low-income to high-income countries. This includes both refugees (including family unification) and economic migrants hoping for higher living standards. There is an important distinction to be made between migration within the EU and between EU and non-EU countries. Within the EU, the "single market" ensures free mobility of workers. When migrants come from outside the EU to an EU country, countries have more freedom to determine their migration rules, which depend on the reason for migration. For refugees, international conventions apply, although countries interpret and administer these rules very differently. This also applies to family unification. For other types of migrants, countries have more discretion, and entry options are closely aligned to labor market skills and options.

Empirical evidence does not give clear support for the magnet hypothesis. Migration pressure is high across most of western Europe, despite very different welfare models. However, an important distinction must still be made between *ex ante* and *ex post* implications. The magnet hypothesis refers to the *ex ante* situation, in which a destination country is chosen by migrants. Even if migrants do not make such deliberations, choosing destination countries without any concern for welfare arrangements, there is an *ex post* issue. What are the options, once in a given country? If immigrants from low-income countries tend to have lower qualifications and thus lower employment rates than the rest of the population, then the financial viability of the model is affected. As explained above, the Nordic welfare model is an employment model. It is even possible that the structure of extended welfare models contributes to making it more difficult for such immigrants to find employment, as discussed below.

First, a look at the data in Figure 7.2 shows employment rates for natives and for immigrants from outside the then EU28 for the four largest Nordic countries, along with the EU averages – with data for women and men. Two comparisons are possible. The first is a level comparison of the employment rates of immigrants from outside the EU28 across countries. The other is a relative comparison: How large is the difference between the employment rates for natives and immigrants from outside EU28 countries in various countries? It is evident from the data that the answers to these questions are very different. The level of employment rates for immigrants – women and men – in the Nordic countries is similar to the level in other EU countries. Considering the gaps, one finds that they are much larger for the Nordic countries than for other EU countries, especially for women. This is crucial, since the employment gaps have important public finance implications.

* Gives the un-weighted average employment rate for the Nordic countries (excluding Iceland) and the EU average based on country of birth. Natives are persons born in the respective EU countries; outside EU28 are persons born outside of the EU28. The data applies to 2019

Figure 7.2 Employment rates and migration, Nordic countries and EU average

a) Male *

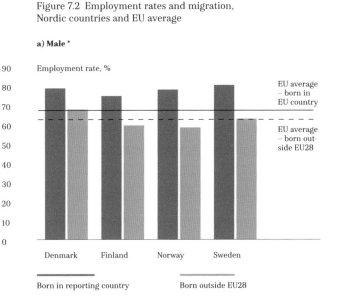

Born in reporting country   Born outside EU28

b) Female *

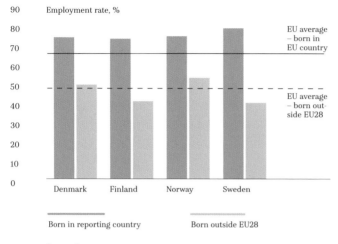

90   Employment rate, %

EU average
– born in
EU country

EU average
– born out-
side EU28

Denmark   Finland   Norway   Sweden

Born in reporting country   Born outside EU28

Source: Eurostat

Numerous studies have analyzed how immigration affects public finances. The overall lesson is that it is very difficult to make generalizations. Immigrants are very heterogeneous along many dimensions, which cannot meaningfully be condensed into one conclusion. What can be concluded, however, is that the public finance consequences of migration depend on the employment rates of various groups of immigrants compared to those of the population at large (the gaps) – which is not surprising, given the properties of the welfare models discussed in Chapter 4. Groups of immigrants that have employment rates below the average affect public finances negatively, and vice versa. Therefore, immigration from high-income countries (which will include a higher share of migrant workers, students, well-educated people) tends to have a positive effect on public finances, while immigration from low-income countries (which will include more asylum seekers and people seeking family reunification, with lower qualifications) tends to worsen public financ-

90

es. While similar effects are seen in countries with leaner welfare states, the effects are obviously stronger in more extended welfare states, since most people without a job will be entitled to some form of "transfer income" and the tax burden on earned income is high. Therefore, a large influx of immigrants with difficulty finding employment challenges the financial viability of the welfare state.

Could the structure of the Nordic welfare model, in itself, be an impediment to employment for some immigrants? The Nordic countries have relatively high minimum wages and a compressed wage structure, and they have no "working poor," so that is not an option. As a consequence, there are relatively high qualification requirements to find a job, and few low-skilled jobs. Migrants from low-income countries typically have low levels of education or lack experience relevant to the Nordic labor markets, and therefore their employment prospects are not good.

In addition, the reference point for labor market participation is high, for both men and women. Therefore, even though the employment rates for various groups of immigrants are not particularly low in absolute terms, the employment gaps are large. This reflects the generally high employment rates for natives (as the welfare model is an "employment model"), and the difference is particularly notable for women. In terms of gender roles, differences in cultures and norms can play an important role here. Additionally, there are language barriers, problems in relation to the recognition of foreign qualifications and degrees, and possible discrimination in the labor market. It is also possible that the incentive effects differ: If social transfers are seen relative to living standards in immigrants' home countries, the urge to find a job may be less strong.

Migration is a particularly sensitive issue. The Nordic countries have traditionally been very open, and in other respects they are known for having relatively liberal views on the way people live their lives. The challenges raised by immigration are complicated. There is a conflict between ensuring higher employment rates for immigrants, and not accepting, for instance, lower minimum wages. There is also vigorous debate about whether migrants should have the same entitlements in the welfare system as natives. On the one hand, it could be argued that it is reasonable for migrants to have less generous entitlements, since they have contributed less to the system. On the other hand, this challenges social inclusion and redistribution, which are primary objectives of the welfare state.

Among the Nordic countries, Denmark has taken the most drastic initiatives on immigration. These apply to both entitlement and entry rules.

First, immigration rules have been tightened. International conventions and EU rules limit the room to maneuver, but the country has adopted new, stricter rules, particularly on family unification. For voluntary migrants from outside the EU, there are now selection criteria that depend on qualifications, job opportunities, and so on. The latter follows an international trend, and there is a "race to the top" to attract the best-qualified labor.

Second, there have been several changes in the social safety net, prompted by immigration issues. The Danish welfare model builds on the principle of universality; that is, equal rights for all, independent of past history (employment, tax payments, and so on). This remains the same for public welfare services, but the coverage from the social safety net has been changed. The core element of the social safety net is the so-called social assistance, providing a floor for economic support to all those unable to support themselves and their families (see Chapter 3). There is now a residence principle that defines eligibility: Full "social rights," including the right to receive social assistance, are attained after residence in Denmark for 9 out of the last 10 years. If an individual does not fulfill these requirements, they are entitled to a different transfer income ("start aid" or "introduction benefit"), which is roughly half the value of social assistance. Eligibility for social assistance also includes requirements related to past employment, which may be more difficult to meet for immigrants. Although these conditionalities do not achieve a complete screening, since they also affect Danes returning after extended periods abroad, they do have the largest effect on groups of immigrants with a low employment rate and thus a high propensity to receive social assistance. This is a qualitative change, implying a departure from universalistic principles.

Mobility and migration also bring about problems that arise because countries pursue different welfare models. This issue is visible within the EU as a consequence of the single market, which has free labor mobility as a cornerstone. Such mobility allows labor to move depending on job and wage opportunities, which contributes to making economic development more similar across EU countries, and thereby potentially strengthens flexibility and adjustability. But it also challenges welfare and labor arrangements like those in the Nordic countries.

The single market has induced worker mobility, as was the intended consequence of EU enlargement, but it has also raised problems. One urgent issue is to ensure compliance with labor market and tax rules. Another, and more problematic, question is whether migrant workers can underbid national labor standards. Even though, in principle, migrant workers must be offered the same conditions as domestic workers, there are various ways to circumvent this, for example by posting workers intended for "temporary" work tasks, in which case their home country's rules apply. Danish unions are therefore concerned that migrant workers may undermine collectively bargained outcomes and trigger "race to the bottom" mechanisms.

A particularly controversial issue is the universal "state child subsidy," for which all parents are eligible, and which is not offered by all EU countries. According to EU regulations, a migrant worker who leaves their family in their home country is eligible for the subsidy, even if the children are not living in Denmark. While the export of such benefits is not large in quantitative terms, it has become a showcase of how EU rules do not properly take differences in welfare systems into account. Since the aim of the subsidy is to ensure social inclusion for children (with levels determined by the cost of living in the country paying the subsidy), it is very controversial that children who are not living in that country are subsidized.

The Nordic welfare model was not carved in stone at some historical moment. It has been continuously adapted to reflect changes in society, although the overarching goals, such as equal opportunities and egalitarian outcomes centered on a large public sector, have characterized the Nordic model all along. There has been an understanding of the need to adapt arrangements to new circumstances, although reforms have, in some cases, been delayed. In the future there will be a continued need for adaptation, and one of the potential drivers is globalization. It remains to be seen whether adaptation will also be possible in the years to come, or whether particular countries with large public sectors will face significant pressures from globalization.

Chapter 8.

The wealth dilemma

There are never-ending discussions about the quality and extent of public welfare services, not least publicly run schools, healthcare, and childcare. It may seem paradoxical that it is so difficult to make ends meet for the welfare state in affluent societies like the Nordics. Nevertheless, the continuous worries about the ability to finance the welfare state are often at the top of the political agenda.

Common sense suggests that when society becomes richer, it should become easier to solve economic problems in general, and the financing of the welfare state in particular. However, things may not be that simple, for several reasons.

Consider first how economic growth driven by higher productivity affects public finances. When income grows, tax revenue also increases for unchanged tax rates. Roughly put, tax revenue will grow at the same rate as incomes. What happens to public expenditures? As discussed in Chapter 3, the public sector basically has two types of expenditures: wage expenditures to public employees, and various forms of transfers. When productivity increases, private sector wages grow, and wages in the public sector will have to grow on a par. If public wages lag behind private wages, it will be increasingly difficult for the public sector to recruit workers. Empirical evidence also shows that the average private wage growth and public wage growth are the same. Hence, higher productivity growth leads to a proportional increase in this expenditure item for unchanged public activities. What about transfers? If transfer recipients are to benefit from the improving living standards, transfers will have to increase proportionally to private wages. If they do not, there will be a widening difference in living standards, leading to more inequality in society. Hence, for an unchanged distributional profile, this expenditure component also increases proportionally to private wages. Summing up, to a first approximation, both tax revenue and public expenditures will grow in parallel to private wage (productivity) growth, and therefore the effect on the budget is neutral.

The basic insight is that if the provision of services and the distributional profile are to remain unchanged, then growth does not automatically create maneuvering room in the public budget. While this argument is presented here in a very stylized way, detailed analyses confirm the basic insight – that economic growth does not automatically make political prioritizations easier.

On second thought, this insight makes intuitive sense. It is not apparent that it should be any easier to be a politician today than it was, say, two or three decades ago.

Actually, economic growth and progress put the public sector under pressure. Service provision is an essential element of the Nordic welfare model. This includes daycare, education (ranging from primary schooling to further education), healthcare systems, old-age care, and so on. Two things characterize these provisions, namely that the standards offered should be "contemporary" and meet the requirements of most people, and that they are tax-financed. Somewhat paradoxically, it may be more difficult to reach these objectives in a situation where productivity growth makes room for improvements in living standards. This is due to both a cost effect and a demand effect, as discussed below.

While the demographic challenge is primarily a question of changes in the quantitative dimension (fewer individuals of working age, increased number of elderly people), the type of challenge known as the "wealth dilemma" addresses qualitative dimensions of the Nordic welfare model. The problem is the ability to provide (and finance) welfare services that meet the needs and requirements of most people. Since economic growth and development create new opportunities, this is a moving target. To reach welfare state objectives, publicly provided services must remain able to meet contemporary standards in the future. It is not sufficient merely to ensure the same standards that exist today. The standards people expect at schools and hospitals today are very different from what was considered acceptable in the 1960s, or even the 1990s. In this discussion, it is important to keep in mind that "wealth dilemma" problems arise due to progress and improvements in society. There is scope for improvements, so the question is how to distribute and allocate these improvements.

Baumol and Wagner

The Nordic welfare model is facing a wealth dilemma, where financial strains on welfare arrangements may develop precisely because society at large is experiencing continuous increases in income and standards of living, due to higher productivity.

The production of services may suffer from what is known as "Baumol's cost disease."[21] While productivity increases steadily for standard goods (like food and manufactured goods), productivity growth is lower or absent in service production. This applies, in particular, to activities

21.
See Baumol, W. J., & Brown, W. G. (1966). *Performing Arts: The economic dilemma*. The Twentieth Century Fund

that are intensive in human interaction, like care-giving. The nature of the activity is at the root of the problem; not whether it is produced in the private or the public sector. Since wage developments are driven by the general level of productivity increases, and since they have to be fairly similar across different sectors to recruit workers, it follows that the relative costs of producing services tend to increase over time. Given that the welfare state is a provider of essential services like education and healthcare, there is an inevitable tendency for costs to increase, even when standards remain unchanged.

Then there is "Wagner's law," which says that the demand for some services has an "income elasticity" above one; that is, the demand increases more than proportionally to an increase in income (for given prices). This tendency is associated with Adolph Wagner, who as early as 1883 predicted that services (and the public sector more generally) would increase in relative importance as economies become richer. Health is usually considered the prime example of a service area with a high "income elasticity." Reducing morbidity and mortality is valued highly by most people, and when more basic needs are satisfied, health improvements attain higher priority. This tendency is also spurred on by new possibilities, as the life sciences continue to make advances in terms of new and better treatments for various diseases. When such new treatments are feasible, there is also an expectation that the public healthcare system should provide it. If not, the system would fail to deliver services that live up to contemporary standards and meet the needs of most citizens. The public healthcare system need not be at the frontier of medical science, but it must follow close behind. Moreover, with more educated citizens, the demand for publicly provided services may increase, since public solutions are challenged by well-informed users, who wish for adjustment and flexibility (one size does not necessarily fit all).

The main source of financing of the welfare state is (direct or indirect) taxation of labor income, as seen in Chapter 3. If higher income and wealth induce people to demand more leisure (a shorter working week, longer vacations, earlier retirement), then total working hours decrease, which in turn reduces the tax base. The ability of the current tax system to finance welfare arrangements may therefore dwindle as productivity increases. The trend increase in leisure observed in most OECD countries may be interpreted as revealing its high income elasticity.

In short, a wealth dilemma arises for the welfare state as society gets richer: Services may become more expensive or be more in demand, and the financing base may shrink due to decreasing individual working hours.

The public provision of services is ultimately a political decision. Therefore, in principle, it is possible for policy-makers to defy the Baumol and the Wagner effects by not accommodating these pressures. However, this would leave an increasing wedge between the services provided by the welfare state and the needs, requirements, and expectations of the population. It violates the premise of publicly provided service standards meeting the demands of the majority and not needing to be supplemented. Gradually, this may lead to increasing dissatisfaction with public solutions, and may eventually erode the support for the welfare state.

The drivers behind the wealth dilemma are not new. However, in the past they were less visible because fiscal space to accommodate them was created, among other things via tax increases, and also by expanding the labor supply (not least through female labor force participation) and benefiting from a demographic tailwind (many young people entering the labor market). In a forward-looking perspective, the picture is quite different, and the wealth dilemma becomes more visible alongside improvements in living standards and the availability of new options.

How to cope with the wealth dilemma?

This seems to leave a conundrum: Either fundamental principles of the welfare state have to be given up,
or taxes have to rise significantly. The following argues
that neither needs to be the case, and that it is possible
to maintain the fundamental principles underlying welfare services in the welfare state: universal access to tax-
financed services of contemporary standards.

Baumol's cost disease is not a natural law in the
sense that it or its consequences cannot be affected. To
discuss the implications and possibilities for adjustment
induced by Baumol's cost disease and technological progress, it is useful to begin by looking at one of the examples
Baumol used to explain the cost disease, namely music.
Take live music in the form of a Beethoven string quartet.
At the time it was composed, in the early nineteenth century, it took four musicians, say, 40 minutes to play. Today,
it still takes 40 minutes to play the quartet. Disregarding
all other aspects (transport, organization of concerts, re-
hearsals, and so forth), productivity is unchanged in terms
of labor input – so the output to input ratio is constant.
However, the cost of producing music has increased, since
wages for musicians have increased, due to general productivity growth and thus general wage increases in society. Compared to food or clothing, the cost or price of
producing that particular piece of music has increased significantly, but it is still affordable. If a person had to work,
say, 3 hours to afford a ticket to the concert in the early
nineteenth century, it would also correspond to 3 hours of
work today. Meanwhile, the relative price has increased –
today's concert-goer can acquire many more food items or
manufactured goods for the price of a concert ticket. The
relative price increase may induce some people to shift
demand away from live concerts, not because they are un-

affordable, but because other spending items have higher priority.

Although productivity in the live performance of a Beethoven quartet cannot be increased without compromising the product, substitutes have been developed. Via inventions, from the gramophone, through fragile "78"s, LPs, tape recordings, and CDs to the streaming of music, access to music has become available at very low prices. More people can afford to listen to immensely more music today than in the late nineteenth century. These ways of listening to and enjoying music are not perfect substitutes for a live concert, but they are close. And they may have other advantages: You can listen to the Beethoven piece when and where you want to, and swiftly change to one of your other favorite composers or bands. The fact that the demand for such alternatives is high shows that customers find these alternatives to live concerts attractive.

This example has several implications that hold importance for the public provision of services. Two, in particular, are worth discussing further, namely innovations and substitution.

The driver for innovation and product development in private markets is the quest to gain market shares and earn a profit. The inventor who can provide access to music at a lower price, of a higher quality, and/or on more flexible terms creates a market. In the public sector, by definition there is not the same automatic mechanism inducing innovation. There is therefore a fundamental challenge of how to induce innovation in the public production of services. In some cases, innovations relevant for private activities can also be used in the public sector (IT, robot vacuum cleaners, and so on), while in other cases there is a need for genuine innovations directed at the specific publicly provided activity. The latter may suffer from the problem that the public sector tends to be managed through a top-down procedure.

However, there is a further step, namely adapting new ways of producing public services (including the organization of work). This new technique has to be adopted, which again requires political initiative and therefore is often a top-down process. For private services, the process is more straightforward; prices disseminate the signal, and customers decide whether to substitute live concerts for music streaming – a bottom-up procedure. For the public sector, this is more complicated, for several reasons. Top-down procedures are generally less adaptive than bottom-up ones. Moreover, since citizens do not see price/cost signals (they are *not* customers), they will not automatically push for changes, or even find them acceptable. On the contrary, there may be a status-quo bias: Why have robot vacuum cleaners at the nursing home when vacuuming could be done the old-fashioned way, by staff? Why change something citizens have become accustomed to, and which at face value seems to be functioning well? A change can be difficult to implement if it does not have general public acceptance. Finally, reorganizing work within the public sector may be more difficult, due to organizational forms and regulations, and collective agreements may also hamper this, for example in the form of strict rules about which types of labor can perform given tasks.

The solutions known as "welfare technologies" are an important and interesting case when discussing productivity increases in the public sector. "Welfare technology" is a broad term for the use of IT and automated processes in basic service activities like care for the elderly. Such technologies range from equipment that lessens the workload for staff in care institutions, over solutions for monitoring and communication, to aids that compensate for physical disabilities or loss of physical capacity. Such technologies may actually reduce the need for manpower in the provision of welfare services, thereby reducing direct human interaction in such activities. These innovations are often seen as "cold technologies" that replace "warm hands," and consequently they are rarely perceived as close substitutes. However, the comparison is not that simple. These technologies also make it easier for elderly people to stay longer in their own homes, or to manage daily routines by themselves, and therefore they strengthen independence, self-determination, and self-respect among the elderly. Finally, even disregarding such aspects, the question is not that simple, since public funds are not unlimited. Hence, if cost savings are possible, the consequences must be assessed, taking into account the benefits from the alternative use of resources.

The way the public sector is organized is crucial. If the budget procedure is a simple adding-up of costs, it will automatically preserve a "business as usual" procedure, and Baumol's cost disease will be confirmed for sure. To mitigate this, specific actions are required. Productivity in services can be improved. New techniques and ways of organizing work make it possible to lower the cost of producing services, developing close substitutes that are cheaper and offer better solutions. There is room to maneuver. The challenge is to ensure that this room is utilized.

Environmental issues

The list of challenges also includes environmental policies in general, and climate policies in particular. While there are serious global changes pertaining to the climate, and calls for large changes, it is not clear that this puts the Nordic welfare model under any more pressure than other countries with leaner welfare arrangements. Addressing climate issues requires changes in energy sources and production structures. This has two dimensions: the need for policy initiatives, and their consequences for the welfare model.

Inherent in the Nordic model is an ability to solve collective decision problems, and addressing negative externalities in relation to the environment and climate requires this sort of action. In a recent ranking of climate initiatives, Denmark and Sweden appear among the leading countries.[22] This does not imply that policy-making is sufficient to meet climate targets, but it does indicate that policy initiatives are being taken. Irrespective of national or regional progress, this is only a partial step, since the problem is global, and unilateral changes do not matter much unless they trigger similar responses from other countries. However, one argument often advanced is that the front-runners may develop comparative advantages in the new "climate-friendly economy."

From a welfare model perspective, the question is whether climate policies affect the welfare state's ability to achieve its objectives, including the financial viability of the model. The effects on economic activity and thus tax bases are ambiguous. On the one hand, some traditional types of activities would have to be reduced or closed down; on the other hand, new investments in more climate-friendly energy types and production forms are required. There is no clear reason why climate policies should erode the financial viability of the Nordic model.

The most effective way to induce a change in energy sources – and promote the development of alternatives – is to introduce "Pigouvian taxes" (such as a carbon tax) levied on conventional types of energy. Such taxes raise revenue, some of which may be needed for research and investments in alternative energy sources, but they may also increase the fiscal space. The latter effect might be used to counteract some of the distributional consequences of carbon taxes.

22.
See the Climate Performance Index 2021, https://ccpi.org/

Chapter 9.
Conclusions

The relatively favorable performance of the Nordic countries is not the result of a quick fix, but the outcome of a long process of striking a balance between welfare state objectives and economic performance. Over time, the Nordics have seen good times and bad, and numerous reforms have been implemented.

The model is not static but continuously adapts to changes in society and the economy, even while the overall objectives remain the same. The welfare state has been designed to balance concerns for economic performance on the one hand, and, on the other, public provision of welfare services and the pursuit of egalitarian outcomes. The experience of the Nordic countries also shows that policy choices are possible even in an era of globalization.

Two points are particularly important when considering the Nordic model. Firstly, while the public sector is large, the private sector is relatively liberal, so the model does not pit "politics against markets." Secondly, welfare arrangements have a strong and active focus on supporting labour market participation and human capital acquisition. Since the financial viability of the welfare model ultimately depends on maintaining a high employment level in the private sector, the conflict between welfare objectives and economic performance is not as stark as it may first appear.

The Nordic countries face a number of challenges, some global and others specific to that particular welfare model. It is an open question whether the properties and track record of the Nordic model make it easier to handle these policy challenges. On the one hand, experience shows that in the past the Nordic countries have been able to adjust policies so as to maintain their key characteristics. On the other hand, this may also imply that some policy options, which are still open to other countries, have already been deployed (such as tax increases, or increases in female labor force participation). Ultimately, all these things depend on political priorities, and there is no economic argument against the likelihood of maintaining a welfare model of the Nordic type in the future.

Suggestions for further reading

Andersen, T. M., Holmström, B., Honpahoja, S., Korkman, S., Söderström, H. T., & Vartiainen, J. (2007). *The Nordic Model – Embracing globalization and sharing risk*. ETLA.

Atkinson, A. (1999). *The Economic Consequences of Rolling Back the Welfare State*. The MIT Press.

Barr, N. (2020). *The Economics of the Welfare State*. Oxford University Press.

Ocampo, J. A. & Stiglitz, J. E. (Eds.). (2018). *The Welfare State Revisited*. Columbia University Press.

Pestieau, P. & Lefebvre, M. (2018). *The Welfare State in Europe – Economic and Social Perspectives*. Oxford University Press.

References

Andersen, T. M. (2015). *The Welfare State and Economic Performance*. Bilaga Långtidsutredningen 2015, SOU 2015:53, Ministry of Finance, Stockholm.

Andersen, T. M., Bergman, U. M., & Hougaard Jensen, S. E. (Eds.). (2015). *Reform Capacity and Macroeconomic Performance in the Nordic Countries*. Oxford University Press.

Andersen, T. M., Holmström, B., Honpahoja, S., Korkman, S., Söderström, H. T., & Vartiainen, J. (2007). *The Nordic Model – Embracing globalization and sharing risk*. ETLA.

Andersen, T. M. & Molander, P. (Eds.). (2003). *Alternatives for Welfare Policies – Coping with Internationalization and Demographic Changes*. Cambridge University Press.

Atkinson, A. (1999). *The Economic Consequences of Rolling Back the Welfare State*. The MIT Press.

Barr, N. (2001). *The Welfare State as Piggy Bank – Information, Risk, Uncertainty and the Welfare State*. Oxford University Press.

Buchanan, J. M. & Musgrave, R. A. (1999). *Public Finance and Public Choice – Two Contrasting Visions of the State*. The MIT Press.

Esping-Andersen, G. (1990). *The Three Worlds of Welfare Capitalism*. Princeton University Press

Lindbeck, A. (1997). The Swedish experiment. *Journal of Economic Literature, 35(3),* 1273–1319.

Lindbeck, A., Molander, P., Persson, T., Petersen, O., Sandmo, A., Swedenborg, B., & Thygesen, N. (1993). *Options for Economic and Political Reform in Sweden*. Stockholm - International Economic Studies.

Lundberg, E. (1985). The Rise and Fall of the Swedish Model. *Journal of Economic Literature, 23,* 1–36.

Lindert, P. H. (2004). *Growing Public – Social Spending and Economic Growth Since the Eighteenth Century.* Cambridge University Press.

Moene, K. O. (2010). Floating High – How the Nordic Model Combines Capitalist Dynamics and Worker Security. In O. Molven (Ed.), *Healthcare, Welfare and Law.* Gyldendal Akademisk.

Moene, K. O. (2016). Reinventing Social Democratic Development – Insights from Indian and Scandinavian Comparisons. *NIAS – Nordic Institute of Asian Studies, 198(7).*

Ocampo, J. A. & Stiglitz, J. E. (Eds.). (2018). *The Welfare State Revisited.* Columbia University Press.

Okun, A. (1975). *Equality and Efficiency: The Big Tradeoff.* Brooking Institution Press.

Pestieau, P. & Lefebvre, M. (2018). *The Welfare State in Europe – Economic and Social Perspectives.* Oxford University Press.

Sandmo, A. (1998). The Welfare State: A Theoretical Framework for Justification and Criticism. *Swedish Economic Policy Review, 5(1),* 11–33.

Sinn, H. W. (2003). *The New Systems Competition.* Blackwell.

Valkonen, T. & Vihriälä, V. (Eds.). (2014). The Nordic Model – Challenged but Capable of Reform. *TemaNord, 531.*